emerging
worship

emerging
worship

Becoming Part of the Sound and Song of Heaven

Roland
Worton

DESTINY IMAGE® PUBLISHERS, INC.

P.O. Box 310, Shippensburg, PA 17257–0310

*"Speaking to the Purposes of God for this Generation
and for the Generations to Come."*

This book and all other Destiny Image, Revival Press, Mercy Place, Fresh Bread, Destiny Image Fiction, and Treasure House books are available at Christian bookstores and distributors worldwide.

For a U.S. bookstore nearest you, call 1–800–722–6774.

For more information on foreign distributors, call 717–532–3040.

Or reach us on the Internet at www.destinyimage.com.

ISBN 10: 0–7684–2698–7
ISBN 13: 978–0–7684–2698–4

For Worldwide Distribution, Printed in the U.S.A.

1 2 3 4 5 6 7 8 9 10 11 / 12 11 10 09 08

Dedication

I dedicate this book to my two sons of power and favor—Caleb and Judah. You are voices to your generation and to the emerging breed of Soundforgers in the nations who are laying down their sound and song to release Heaven's.

Acknowledgments

My incredible wife, Shirin, you are gifted and wonderful. Thank you for allowing me the flexibility to write and for your powerful intercession over our lives and call.

Mom, Dad, and Lee—for your love, consistency and encouragement.

Terry and Susan Moore, our Senior Pastors, thank you for believing in us and investing in us in so many ways. You are true apostolic leaders.

To the spiritual parents who have invested and impacted me so powerfully—Jean and Elmer Darnall, Alan and LaDonna Elliot, Sam and Lyn Yeghnazar, Rod and Julie Anderson, and Doug Stringer.

Cindy Jacobs—you are an amazing woman of God who has pioneered, modeled, sacrificed, laughed and cried your way into the nations. You have been positioned at pivotal junctions in our lives, including this one. Thank you for fulfilling your call and for your impact upon our lives.

Sojourn Elders and Pastors—I love this team.

My assistant Cheryl Haun—thank you for your faithful, consistent behind-the-scenes work for this book and the ministry. Let the BD anointing rise!

Our personal intercessors, Roxanne Buchschacher and Brenda

Callahan, for your heart and commitment to our family and this project. Go daughters of thunder! Russell Square is calling.

Nathan Hudson—thanks for letting me father you—you have an amazing future.

The Destiny Image team—for running with this message and allowing it to go out undiluted.

To all who provided advice and feedback in the early stages of the book. Thanks particularly to Beth Clark, Mary Forsythe, and Brenda Callahan.

Alan Coulter—for lending yourself to help me formulate the first stage of this project, you have become a friend and an encourager.

Diane Fink, Nancy Cobb, and Nonnie McVeigh—for bringing prophetic words from Heaven at crucial times.

To the family and staff at Sojourn, ICF London, Elam, Prayer for the Nations, and Bridgeway—you are all incredible!

Ministry supporters—thank you for sowing into Soundforgers—you are helping me raise and impact a generation.

With prophetic insight, sound biblical foundation, and cutting-edge clarity, Roland Worton charts a course for the current transition through God's Spirit in the realm of corporate worship. Hearing the sound from Heaven for this hour, Roland offers not only an understanding of apostolic worship, but the practicalities of moving into it as well. You will be inspired and challenged as you read!

Jane Hansen, President/CEO
Aglow International

Roland Worton has approached the evolving reformation of apostolic worship in a very thoughtful and insightful way. He does not communicate to us merely from theory, but as a practitioner of the message. Though a humble servant, he exudes authority and confidence in the One he worships. I believe he has tapped into an understanding of the presence and power of the Spirit that brings a fresh revelation of Christ through apostolic worship. It awakened my heart with a renewed passion to dwell with the King, empowered by the authority of His manifest presence.

Doug Stringer, President,
Somebody Cares International

My wife, Julie, and I had the privilege of working intimately with Roland for several years, and in many respects he is a spiritual son to us. What is written in *Emerging Worship* is most definitely not theory, but rather first-hand experience with the accompanying results that only Heaven can release. Roland is in many ways a true forerunner in prophetic and apostolic worship. He understands that the closest relationship to the prophet is the psalmist and carries out his calling with shocking integrity that freezes the plans of God's enemies. Leaders, as you read this book, receive the wisdom that will bring release and cause your church to come up to new levels in the Spirit. Musicians, receive the revelation of intentional humility and aggressive dependency upon the Spirit of God that Roland models and communicates so well. The work of the Spirit in this book is essential to bringing corporate release in Davidic worship to the Church. If received, this book will release the reader from individual anointings to corporate anointings, which opens a whole new dimension of spiritual breakthrough. There are worship leaders, and then there are leaders who worship. Roland is a leader.

Rod Anderson,
Cofounder/Director, Prayer for the Nations, England
Senior Pastor, Commonwealth Church,
Mayfair, London, England

During the '60s I worked for Brian Epstein and the Beatles. By the late '90s, I was leading a Strategic Prayer School in Westminster and Roland was an answer to my prayer for a Psalmist, who could bring God's heart and Presence. Roland pioneers in worship in the most incredible heartfelt way as he interprets what God is saying and turns it into songs from Heaven.

This book will capture your attention, and equip you with what the Spirit of God is doing among a new breed of young Christians beyond church worship as we have known it before. God is raising up warriors of love, and worshipers in war with revelation to step out further, who will stand strong in the spiritually new, so that others can find God more easily for themselves. This new breed of extravagant worshiper will glean much from this book and in applying what Roland has lived out, their influence will be felt—and societies will change.

We are living in exciting days when something supernatural is happening through music, bringing closure to the sixties. Today's rising generation is being given many new beginnings. This book is here in perfect timing to see the recovery God is bringing to today's youth in the nations. Read it—do what it teaches, and you will see Heaven break through into your life.

Julie Anderson, Cofounder

Prayer for the Nations, England

First, I want to recommend Roland Worton. He is a true worshiper who not only is gifted and talented but lives for Jesus and the Kingdom. Having had the privilege of working with him and serving as his pastor for the past five years, I have observed his life. His personal walk as a husband, father, and pastor reflects Christ. He has been a blessing to me and the church we serve.

Second, I want to recommend *Emerging Worship*. God is raising up a new breed of prophetic and apostolic worshipers to lead His Body into new dimensions of His presence. Roland clearly articulates what this looks like and how we can personally move into it. You will be encouraged and inspired as you read this book.

Terry Moore, Senior Pastor
Sojourn Church, Texas

In this strategic season God is releasing a powerful dominion author-ity through His Church that will shift nations and generations. This move of the Spirit is indelibly linked to a new sound of the Spirit of God coming forth through the hearts and mouths of His worshipers. It has the ability to translate the sounds coming from God's throne in Heaven to penetrate the kingdoms of the earth and bring revolu-tionary change. In *Emerging Worship,* Roland Worton not only defines *what* is happening in this new release of the Spirit, but *how* we can partner with the Lord to cause it to happen in our own spheres of influence in the earth realm. This book is a powerful tool, which every leader should read and every worshiper should live.

Jane Hamon, Co-Senior Leader
Christian International Family Church

We have entered the time when the sound created in worship has never been more critical. The sound can penetrate the spirit of man, break through demonic forces and atmospheres, and release Heaven on earth. It can disrupt the sound of false religion. Roland has cap-tured in this book what I believe is vital to worshipers in this hour. This book is cutting edge, a voice crying in the wilderness to the new breed of worship leaders and worshipers arising.

Barbara J. Yoder, Senior Pastor and Lead Apostle
Shekinah Christian Church

Roland Worton offers a carefully crafted contribution to our understanding of the place of worship in this important season of transition. I pray that this book will impact the contemporary worship, prophetic, and intercessory scene to the glory of God and the greater manifestation of his Kingdom in the world.

Roger Mitchell
Passion, United Kingdom

Roland Worton has fresh, powerful insight on prophetic and apostolic worship in a way that I have not seen from other leaders. I was touched and received fresh vision as an intercessory leader both personally and as a prayer leader while reading this revelatory book. I highly recommend it for any believer, regardless of age, and think it should be in the library of all Christians in the Body of Christ.

Dr. Cindy Jacobs
Generals International
Reformation Prayer Network

I am exicited about this book. While we have enjoyed worship in its present form, we've seen litle of heaven's invasion of earth in the Experience. *Emerging Worship* is to change that trend, as Roland Worton has truly captured the heart of God in this matter. The effect of *Emerging Worship* can touch every segment of society. I highly recommend this book to all believers.

Bill Johnson
Senior Pastor—Bethel Church, Redding, CA
Author—*When Heaven Invades Earth* and *Face to Face with God*

Contents

Chapter 1

Soundforgers

Forge— to shape by heating and hammering, a furnace used for heating. To form or make, to fashion, to invent or devise.[1]

Early in 2000 the Lord gave me a vision that arrested my heart and captured my attention. I believe that it speaks to an emerging breed and the war for their destinies in these days:

Musicians were hidden away in worn leather tents set in various locations in a barren wasteland. As an impending storm blew in, they worked intently and actively with materials that were not clearly iden-tifiable to the natural eye—articles that I did not have a description for. I knew instinctively that these substances were spiritual in nature and were being pieced together in various combinations with an emphasis upon forging sound. I also knew that through their encounters with the Father, many of these young musicians had previously glimpsed what they were looking to create; however the sound that emerged from the dwellings was muffled and stifled. As I watched, an angelic being with a trumpet stood and played over the earth, suddenly awakening these

hidden musicians again to a greater awareness of the Father's presence. Freshly saturated, the sounds of Heaven were now beginning to
be discovered as they continued to work creatively.

Suddenly a sound broke from one of the tents that caused a great
shaft of liquid light to be released upward and connect to what was
an already open Heaven; it was a sound that literally split the sky and
shook the earth. As I continued to watch, the Father sent companies
of angels to observe these sons of men, to see who could and would
continue to carry and represent the sound. These angels celebrated
each discovery. I then saw tests and seasons being set before these
Soundforgers that would offer lifestyle choices—each with unique
assignments and challenges. I knew that the outcome of these tests
in their personal lives would be important ingredients that would
help continually shape the music that came from their lives. Love for
the lost, compassion, purity, humility, and *no reputation* would come
together to form a sound of authority and dominion that would be
used as a weapon against all that was unlawful on the earth.

This is the time for the emergence of a new breed of *Soundforger.*

They are already here and no longer satisfied to sweetly sing the
songs of yesterday's season or to pacify the call to an extravagant pursuit
of God for observance to religiosity—but are hearing the piercing cry of
their Warrior-Bridegroom, Jesus, who is making declarations of change
over the earth. Hidden and hearing, they are locking into the Kingdom
DNA that has been deposited in them. They are forging and emerging
within a distinct spiritual climate, carrying distinct weaponry and
becoming increasingly aware of their distinct purpose—to see the
sounds and songs of Heaven released into the Earth for transformation.

GLOBAL CONTEXT

There is a growing need to perceive and to understand the multi-faceted role of these Soundforgers, and within the current climate of praise and worship, experience the equipment that God has deposited and is releasing. We are poised to reclaim and receive the Father's inheritance in these *Heaven-hearers*, and it is crucial to understand the context within which this emergence is taking place.

The corporate gathering of the Body of Christ is being redefined by the Holy Spirit. We are finding 24/7 houses of prayer emerging in the nations, an increase in the recognition and activation of the *city-wide* as well as the *local* expression of the Church. Extended worship times devoid of an agenda other than pursuing Heaven, and many massive, as well as grass roots prayer incentives, are being implemented to see Heaven invade earth as well as monumental shifts in times of national and international crises.

We are also in the early stages of a reformation in the mobilization of the entire Church as activated God-carriers. It is the day of the saints and radical restorative and revival anointings are being released over the Body of Christ all over the nations of the earth. We are being equipped as a no-reputation task force to move to new levels in every arena and strata of life outside of the four walls of the Church. Saturated with the presence, wisdom and favor of God, we understand more than ever that we are called to impact every sphere of society. The seven mountains or pillars of education, government, religion, business, family, media, and arts and entertainment are being impacted as marketplace revolutionaries are recognized by the Body, and activated and released by the Holy Spirit.[2]

Alongside this, *business-as-missions* is exploding in the nations at an unprecedented rate as the Body of Christ moves from sending missionaries only to planting profit-producing businesses in unreached regions. The transformation of communities through Christ-centered business initiatives is a significant part of the Kingdom dynamic that God is releasing in this season.

Another dimension of the current spiritual climate in which these Soundforgers are emerging is the recognition of the 'Kingdom of God' and the restoration of the five-fold ministry gifts (see Eph. 4:11) to the Church like never before. The First-Century Church clearly operated with Kingdom understanding and functioned with and related to apostles, prophets, pastors, teachers and evangelists. It is clearly a season of the alignment with the Kingdom of God and the integration of the five-fold gifts into the way that we operate. Whether we entitle individuals or not, the emergence of the function of Ephesians 4:11 government in the global Church is undeniable.[3]

THREE DIMENSIONS

Alongside these global trends, corporate worship is also emerging with recognizable characteristics. There are many valid expressions. Some have been engraved into the fabric of the Church for centuries; others are current rediscoveries of ancient wells, and some are new and now—never heard before. We are going to discuss and focus on three dynamic aspects of present day worship that we see emerging. We will unpack each one individually and explore various issues concerning their functions. Let me briefly define these three dimensions:

- Priestly Worship—functions from **Earth to Heaven** and is the foundation of worship from us to God.

- Prophetic Worship—functions in **releasing revelation** and is a vehicle that carries the voice of God.

- Apostolic Worship—functions from **Heaven to Earth** and carries within its sound and content the authority of God.

RESTORATION OF THE TABERNACLE OF DAVID

The establishing of the Tabernacle of David in the Old Testament as a radical model for corporate worship holds crucial keys for us today in seeing the fullness God has for worship. Over 3,000 years ago, the multidimensional expression of priestly, prophetic, and apostolic worship was a daily occurrence in Israel. We see this reflected in the multifaceted book of Psalms. Some of these ancient songs lend themselves to tender, intimate offerings to the Father and others are governing declarations over nations and the enemies of God. This God-music, operating out of His Presence, was in place 24/7 under the direction of King David, our blueprint Soundforger.

Passionate worshipers are recapturing Tabernacle worship today, and God is now positioning these men and women to bring their activated weaponry into the fight over regions and nations. Just as in the days of David, God is raising those all over the Earth who will forge, carry and release the sounds and songs of Heaven.

There are several promises in the Word of God that we can lock into regarding the restoration of Tabernacle worship in the nations:

> *On that day I will raise up the Tabernacle of David which has fallen down, and repair its damages; I will raise up its ruins, and rebuild it as in the days of old; that they may possess the remnant of Edom, and all the Gentiles who are called by My name* (Amos 9:11-12 NKJV).

> *After this I will return and will rebuild the tabernacle of David, which has fallen down; I will rebuild its ruins, and I will set it up; so that the rest of mankind may seek the Lord, even all the Gentiles who are called by My name* (Acts 15:16-17 NKJV).

This speaks of a time, when again, a Tabernacle of worship will be in place that reproduces worship with the same imprint and DNA that David released. The book of Acts echoes this Scripture again within the context of Jesus *fulfilling* the promise. This does not speak of a physical location, but to the truth that the corporate Bride is being built together to become a habitation place for Him that overflows to neighborhoods and nations. It says that God will rebuild it, Jesus has already fulfilled it, and just like everything else He does—it is initiated so that the nations might seek Him and find Him!

Most of us know the story. The ark of God was restored to Israel after being captured by the Philistines for a season and brought back to Jerusalem with passionate celebration by David (see 2 Sam. 6). His extravagant response to the glory of God returning to the land is undignified in the eyes of man. Having learned how to handle the presence of God correctly after the order of God and not man, his affection toward Heaven is unstoppable. The first, new cart symbolizing the best efforts of man to host the presence of God was made to carry the ark but resulted in death and disappointment. Only the consecrated shoulders of a called priesthood who had not presumed but prepared in obedience was ultimately trusted to carry the presence (see 2 Sam. 6:13).

What David instituted here was a massive shift away from what was in place under Mosaic Law. The physical shift into the Tabernacle resulted in continual public praise and worship before God with no veil to hide His presence. Whereas, just a few miles away at Shiloh, priests were still offering regular daily sacrifices before an empty holy of holies. Today God is restoring the heart of passionate worship in the middle of our communities while many of us remain in old patterns that were once life-giving but have now become religious forms devoid of His presence. The issue is not in the style of music played but in the encounter, the interaction with the Holy Spirit, and the extent of life that is released. I have encountered countless life-giving worship experiences that have been centered around ancient hymns. My relationship with God was expanded through the use of these more traditional songs of worship that I was simply not so familiar with. Although I personally prefer and gravitate toward what is more contemporary, the latest songs and sounds do not necessarily carry the life of the Holy Spirit that is needed just because they are the latest and greatest.

David stands as a forerunning model of a New Testament man positioned in the Old Testament. He penned countless songs throughout his lifetime that reveal Him as a passionate man with an enlarged heart after God. He is clearly entrusted with a new form of worship that finds its roots in the desire of man's heart to exist in passionate pursuit of God, and in God's parallel desire to indwell man. First Chronicles chapters 23-25 reveal keys to how this worship operated and models principles for us as David responded to God and appointed teams of musicians and singers.

In First Chronicles 23, after a lifetime of pursuit, old in years, he sets in place this order for worship that we are still unfolding and unlocking in our generation. David appointed and positioned 4,000 Levites to worship God on the instruments that he provided (see 1 Chron. 23:5)—instruments that he had created, to see sounds *forged* that could touch the heart of God and express in sound and rhythm glimpses of who He truly was. They were descendants of the Levitical priesthood (see 1 Chron. 23:24), separated into teams under the life flow of three leaders—Asaph, Jeduthun, and Heman (see 1 Chron. 24:3) and were instructed simply to stand before God each morning and evening to worship (see 1 Chron. 23:30). Two hundred and eighty-eight were set apart for the prophetic, accompanied by instruments (see 1 Chron. 25:1), and some of these clearly prophesied with the instruments themselves (see 1 Chron. 25:3). They were all skilled, trained, moved under the relational supervision of "fathers" and were in multigenerational teams consisting of both teachers and students (see 1 Chron. 25:6-9). From these teams of musicians came the majority of the sounds and songs that were written in the Psalms. Today, just as in the Tabernacle of David, we are called to work with appointed teams of musicians and singers who are consecrated and released as well as skilled and trained.

The combined meanings of the names of David's three—Asaph, Jeduthun, Heman—carry application for God's Soundforgers. The root Hebrew words encapsulate a "faithful, enduring collector of God's thoughts."[4] Present-day psalmists are called primarily to capture and document what God is saying, doing, singing, and sounding! Today, in this generation, we are called to be collectors of Heaven's thoughts and sounds, releasing this new form of worship that was prophesied would be restored. We are releasing that which is already in our spiritual DNA—that which is already here, and just like Jeremiah's fire, is shut up in our bones (see Jer. 20:9).

KEY OF DAVID

Alongside revelation of the Tabernacle of David, Soundforgers are discovering how to carry and use the Key of David in corporate worship.

> *The key of the House of David I will lay on His shoulder; so He shall open, and no one shall shut; and He shall shut, and no one shall open* (Isaiah 22:22 NKJV).

For to us a child is born, to us a Son is given, and the gov-
ernment will be on His shoulders....Of the increase of his
government and peace there will be no end (Isaiah 9:6-7).

Governmental authority has been set upon the shoulders of
Jesus. Biblically, His governmental authority is referred to in many
symbolic ways. It is obviously described here as the Key of David for a
reason. We know that David was personally a "man after God's own
heart" and that by appointment was a king who carried Heaven's
authority and influence (see 1 Sam. 13:14; Acts 13:22). The Key of
David speaks of authority to lock and unlock. The "key" to David's life
was this: out of extravagant intimacy as a man after God's own heart,
he ultimately walked in authority to stand as a giant-slayer and as a
king appointed by the King. The combination of David's cultivated
heart after God and the investment of authority from Heaven qualified him to stand at a point of history and be a vehicle that changed
things forever. He was not used because he had been positioned by
man but because he was positioned by Heaven and created as an
outrageous lover of God and of His ways.

Likewise, generations of sons and daughters have been created
and commissioned to move in the same authority that was bestowed
upon an unlikely group of disciples 2,000 years ago in an upper room.
Jesus handed the Keys of the Kingdom—His authority—to the
Church in the New Testament. Right now, today, He has literally
handed the Key of David to us, His Church in the form of the Keys of
the Kingdom! (See Matt. 16:19.)

Of course, I believe that Isaiah 22:22 is a Messianic prophecy and that the Key of David being set upon Jesus' shoulders speaks of His opening the gateway to relationship with the Father for the nations of the earth and shutting the gates of death and hell. However, in applying the term *Key of David* to music—as David was both King and the Psalmist of Israel—we see a clear picture of governing or apostolic worship. It links together the one man as a type and shadow of Jesus, who carried both the *heart* and the *government* of God. Just as David had a key of intimacy with the Father, so New Testament musicians pick up the Keys of the Kingdom given to them because of relationship with God. A key of governmental authority gives access and opens doors that are normally closed to others.

There is a current need to *define and activate* the authority He has given to God's Soundforgers. In past generations we have walked in the authority of God released through preaching, teaching, counseling, and more recently through gifts of healing and miracles, intercession, prophecy, and five-fold leaders. We also need to walk in a greater measure of revelation regarding the equipment God has deposited within His psalmists and minstrels as they partner with five-fold leadership and the corporate Body in the greater purposes of God. The intimate extravagant worshipers who have touched the heart of their Father and who have seen the fire in the eyes of their Bridegroom are being given authority out of relationship with God to use this Key of David—this key of musical authority.

If David standing in the Old Covenant office of Priest, Prophet, and King released governing declarations in his songs over 3,000 years ago, how much more today in this New Covenant will Jesus, the King of kings, who *holds* the key of David release priestly, prophetic, and governing songs through His Church into the earth. (See Revelation 3:7.)

> And in mercy shall the throne be established: and he shall sit upon it in truth in the tabernacle of David, judging, and seeking judgment, and hasting righteousness (Isaiah 16:5 KJV).

FIVE-FOLD LEADERS

Along with understanding the Tabernacle of David and using the Key of David, the function of five-fold ministry is part of the context in which the new sound is emerging. Many significant books have been written on the function of the five-fold ministry, particularly the office of the apostle and prophet. It is not necessary to outline the key characteristics of them here, but we know with increasing clarity that this is the day of embracing a five-fold leadership paradigm which utilizes all of these people gifts and their function within the Body as seen in the New Testament Church. It is time for a five-fold ministry paradigm to give us context for everything we engage in. In the days of the Tabernacle of David, the ministries of prophet, priest, and king in the Old Testament gave a structure to and a context for leadership. Likewise, today as worshipers and musicians we need an experiential understanding and relationship with the five-fold ministry in order to accurately locate our Kingdom position and function. Barbara Yoder underlines the significance of the current positioning of apostles and prophets:

Apostles and Prophets are arising together for breakthrough. Prophets will perceive and boldly declare the
word of the Lord that releases direction and life. Apostles
will begin to authoritatively move the Church forward
through bold action, releasing great power.... Together
they are about to become the battle-axe that will break
through every barrier.[5]

In order for breakthrough to occur, we must become aligned
with the function of the apostles and prophets. I believe that all born-
again believers, and therefore, all psalmists and minstrels are called
to carry and function in aspects of *apostolic* and *prophetic* anointing
and ministry within their designated spheres of influence. However,
they may not be called and positioned as a governmental gift of
apostle or prophet to the Church as outlined in Ephesians 4:11.

As the prophetic and apostolic in the Body of Christ come
increasingly to the forefront in our society and communities, we need
to understand the ministry function and develop vocabulary for the
parallel and progressive move toward acknowledging and calling
into position both ***prophetic and apostolic worship.*** In using the
term *apostolic worship* I am referring to sounds and songs that literally carry aspects of the government of God within them and often
partner with strategic places of *breaking through* in corporate gatherings and within geographic regions. (Again, in acknowledging that
believers operate in aspects of apostolic anointing I want to clarify
that I am not referring to someone standing in the office of apostle,
although some of them may.) Just as aspects of teaching, Church

doctrine, and the pastoral have flowed through much of our music and songs, so dimensions of both prophetic and apostolic ministry and anointings must operate also. Apostolic worship will increasingly need its own definition. It is *apostolic* because it carries within its sound and content an ability to declare the fullness of Christ, spiritually break through and make a way through uncharted territory—enabling a corporate or geographical shift.

UNDERSTANDING THE SEASON

A transition is taking place in the corporate setting. In worship, we are increasingly moving from dwelling in intimacy to moving into the prophetic and apostolic. Much of our praise and worship has existed in the necessary and Father-centered priestly dimension—the offering of earth to Heaven, the "I love you" of a people captivated and in love with the Creator. In some settings there has been a natural progression into prophetic worship so that now many are comfortable with the release of prophetic revelatory songs in corporate worship. However, there is currently a natural progression into apostolic worship that forerunners have been moving in, but most of our gatherings do not yet have a context for.

Corporate worship that remains *only* in the priestly will sustain a rich devotional dynamic but will often forfeit the momentum to progress forward, possibly remaining self-focused and lacking in all that is available in moving with God. Equally, those who embrace *only* prophetic worship can lose sight of the relational aspect of Father, forfeiting intimacy—seeking to *move* with Him at the expense of *being* with Him. The embracing of apostolic worship adds to our worship experience a dimension of corporate activation and enabling. The governmental anointing and declaration that is released through apostolic worship ensures momentum, change, and alignment that intimate priestly worship alone cannot move us into. These three strands are combining to transform our corporate worship gatherings into purpose-filled encounters. Many of the Psalms begin in a place of reaching out to the Father in lovesick devotion and progress into militant declaration. Jesus spent extended time in intimacy with the Father, and from that place released incredible authority and the *now* of God that healed the terminally ill, raised the dead, and transformed the unlovable.

I want to be clear that I am not endorsing another method of worship that we need to implement in order to be *on target*. Neither am I calling us into another required list of works, but rather highlighting that these three tributaries of the priestly, prophetic and apostolic have always existed in biblical worship since the days of David and are still emerging today. I am not suggesting that all of these aspects of worship would be appropriate in every worship setting; they often stand alone or are interwoven to work together. We are simply in a pivotal place of transition that is requiring definition and permission for a wider context of operation for the way God wants to use music and worship in the corporate setting.

As we stand at the beginning of the 21st century, the Spirit of God is transforming our corporate gatherings into Spirit-led groups who are consistent in the priestly as those that minister to Heaven; dynamic in the prophetic as proclaimers to cities, regions, and nations; and powerful in apostolic authority to see shifts within every sphere of earthly rule. Just as in the vision I described at the beginning of the chapter, God is awakening and raising voices all over the Earth that carry the weapons of the sounds and songs of Heaven into the fight. McManus, in his book *The Barbarian Way*, speaks of a risk-all regenerated generation, which is being identified and called upon:

> …invisible Kingdoms are at war for the hearts and lives of every human being who walks on the face of this Earth. And times of war require barbarians who are willing to risk their life itself for the freedom of others. The irony, of course, is that barbarians are driven away in times of peace—they only disrupt our communities, traditions and sensibilities. It is only in the most desperate of times—times of war and conflict—that these outcasts are welcomed or even invited to return.[6]

Soundforgers are here with voices of strength, voices of truth, voices that are uncompromised, voices that carry life. They may disrupt our traditions and sensibilities if we will let them. Even now, they are being drafted into strategic geographic places of extreme spiritual significance. I know that many of you, or those close to you, have been trained in the wilderness and have been challenged to pay the price of many seasons to be given access to the sounds and songs that expose and devastate fortified places. Because of the intensity of the training, you are not afraid of Goliath, Jezebel, or the religious spirit, but in contrast carry music with an authority in its DNA that demonstrates the Kingdom of God to the ruling systems of the Earth.

Because of these new levels of freedom and Kingdom release, the religious spirit is beginning to manifest in resistance and even antagonism against the emergence of God's government and will continue to do so. Its ancient purpose has always been to extinguish the passionate pursuit of God through the highlighting of minor issues and tradition at the expense of major issues and God's incredible moving in the Earth. The religiosity of modern day Pharisees is given no place where Jesus speaks and the truth sets us free. We will look more at the characteristics of opposing spirits in a later chapter.

It is as though we have been standing in the passing of an era for some time—the kingdom of Saul being removed and the kingdom of David being established (see 2 Sam. 3:1). The form of man's institution is giving way to God's Kingdom. Passivity preserving worship that stands as a pillar in the house of docile and domesticated Christianity is giving way to a fierce fire of extravagant music and governing declaration that burns with the intensity of the One who fuels its flame. Those who have a measure of how things are when He is *everything* are finding their voices in extravagant priestly worship, sharp prophetic revelation, and apostolic power to declare. He is making Himself known in our corporate gatherings.

In this current climate the *now* of God's manifest presence and purpose is taking priority over fixed song lists, man's agendas, and the methods and formulas we have always used. New prophetic and apostolic songs and musical declarations will be given increasing space in the corporate setting in order for the Body to step into and possess what the Father is initiating. It is crucial that emerging Soundforgers understand their call, identity, place, and equipment in the unfolding of history—just as those who were set in place in the Tabernacle. If we do not clearly understand our identity as those called to stand in all that has already been released from Heaven, we will live in a diminished place and forfeit much. Our birthright and call to be dynamic change agents is not negotiable.

By their very equipment, apostolic Soundforgers alongside five-fold governing leaders (see Eph. 4:11) will take entire congregations and gatherings from A to B in the context of worship, causing groups of people to take their place in corporate governing, which will flow out into the streets. Traditional structures of what it means to *"do church"* can no longer house what God wants to do. We live in desperate days where even a small glimpse into our nations and neighborhoods reveals increasing bondage, depression, and disillusionment. The *"real"* Jesus and the *"true"* Church are being revealed, and the Body of Christ is moving into her place of activation for ultimate societal influence and transformation. There is coming a place for the Body of Christ to stand in her God-given promises where the miraculous breaks into every arena of society. When Israel crossed into the Promised Land, the Levitical priesthood stepped into the river ahead of the nation with the presence of God on their shoulders (see Josh. 3:9-17).

They stood while the whole nation passed by.

There is an emerging place for Soundforgers to stand in the flow of the river of God, carrying the presence of Christ on their lives, releasing the sounds and songs of Heaven until the full measure of the Bride has passed. The new emerging breed of Soundforger boldly steps into the river, ahead of the miracle and ahead of the people until the whole nation passes by.

The Spirit of God is currently forming and transforming our current understanding of praise and worship to transition the Body of Christ from standing intimately in the priestly to becoming prophetic proclaimers and apostolic declarers to their cities, nations, and governments. Soundforgers are rising and beginning to step out carrying the Key of David. They are releasing a sound where intimacy, revelation, and declaration marry. How we receive and partner with them on the frontlines of war will determine much as the Body of Christ is released into her multifaceted, dynamic place of promise and destiny.[7]

ENDNOTES

1. *Collins English Dictionary*, Third Edition (Great Britain: Harper Collins Publishers, 1993).

2. The idea that we can view society as seven distinct spheres was communicated in recent years by Bill Bright of Campus Crusade and Loren Cunningham, Youth With a Mission. Lance Wallnau is presently expanding this revelation for further understanding and activation. The teaching series *The Seven Mountain Strategy* (Lance Wallnau Group, Rhode Island) encapsulates the core values of this message.

3. Marked by their influence, pioneering spirit, breadth of oversight, character, and display of the power of God; Rolland and Heidi Baker, Iris Ministries, Mozambique; Sunday Adelaja, Embassy of God,

Ukraine, and Naomi Dowdy, Trinity Church, Singapore are just three of the many widely accepted apostles functioning today.

4. Concept taken from the teaching *The Prophetic Psalmist*, Dan McCollum, Bethel School of the Prophets, August 8, 2006.

5. Barbara J. Yoder, *The Breaker Anointing* (Ventura, CA: Regal Books, 2004), 87.

6. Erwin McManus, *The Barbarian Way* (Nashville, TN: Thomas Nelson Inc., 2005),16.

7. Concepts from this chapter were previously released as an article written by the author, "The Emerging Prophet Musicians," *Cross Rhythms Magazine* (Issue 67, London, UK, 2002), 22, 23.

Forging Sound

In the beginning God created the heavens and the earth. Now the earth was formless and empty, darkness was over the surface of the deep, and the Spirit of God was hovering over the waters. And God said, "Let there be light," and there was light (Genesis 1:1-3).

From the beginning of creation God has commanded order out of chaos—establishing the created out of the *uncreated*. The meaning of the Hebrew word for *formless* means literally, a place of chaos or confusion.[1] The Spirit of God partners with the Father, literally hovering over the pre-formed universe. The root word describing the positioning of the Holy Spirit here means to be moved or affected with feelings of tender love.[2] The Spirit lends Himself to brooding over the Father's intended creation, waiting for the command to release incredible change. In the beginning God *spoke*—what science would call a *sound wave*—and released a word of intent that brought life out of the void.

Today, still resonating with the life of the One who spoke the world into existence, all of creation worships. The Word of God tells us that stars celebrate, rocks cry out, and rivers run with joy (see Ps.

96:11,98:8). All creation sings. Throughout the generations, reclaimed sons and daughters have engaged in this inbuilt default of the Universe. Human beings, unlike other created forms, are made in the image of God—unique in our ability to speak and communicate. To hear the intent of the Father, to forge, and then communicate is our privileged position. The Word actually tells us that *all creation* groans and waits in eager anticipation for the revealing of the sons of God (see Rom. 8:19). (We will talk later about our original job description given to us by the Father in the Garden.)

Soundforgers have always existed—from Jubal, the first musician in the book of Genesis (see Gen. 4:21), to today's 21st-century psalmists who are infusing the atmosphere of Heaven into the earth realm through life-giving songs and sounds. The company of Levites in the Tabernacle off David; Isaac Watts, the 17th-century hymn writer; Count Zinzendorf, founder of the Moravian prayer movement; William Booth, the Salvation Army visionary; and Keith Green, the prophet musician—each carried a distinct sound in their generation that resonated with the heart of Heaven, touched earth, ordered chaos, and stirred the deposits of God in those being raised for Kingdom greatness.

Courage and tenacity to touch the heart of God even in spiritually desolate eras have been a characteristic mark of these Soundforgers throughout history. In A.D. 400, a monastic house of prayer and worship was established by Alexander Akimites in Gorman, at the mouth of the Black Sea. After a seven-year retreat in the desert, Alexander the Sleepless gathered four hundred monks that made up the order of Acoemetae—the sleepless ones. Romans, Greeks, Egyptians, and

Syrians were drawn to Akimites and established prayer watches in their own languages. They launched and sustained constant worship and intercession and are known over 1,600 years later as a pioneer company who set their faces to invade Heaven with Earth and in turn invade Earth through an open Heaven.[3]

The Moravian prayer movement that began in Herrnhut, Germany in 1727, is branded as the model for the contemporary 24/7 resurgence. This community of perpetual prayer and Christ-centred existence, led by Zinzendorf, continued in unbroken worship and intercession for over 100 years. The Moravians were formed into 24 prayer choirs that engaged in daily prayer watches. Radical discipleship also partnered with this unbroken prayer as cell groups met up to three times each day to worship, receive teaching and walk out the call to live for Jesus. Out of this place of unified Heaven-seeking, God unveiled a strong call to missions to Zinzendorf and the Moravians. Recognized as the first large scale Protestant missionary movement, they were the first to send unordained but called people to infuse the Kingdom into many pre-Christian regions.[4] Impacted by the Moravians, Charles Wesley, the brother of the radical reformer John Wesley, wrote hundreds of songs that partnered with the new moves of God that swept across England in the 1700s. In the 1800s, blind from birth, Frances Jane Crosby forged over 8,000 songs in her lifetime in response to the glorious One she saw with eyes of the Spirit. The singing sisters of the Welsh revival[5] engaged in spontaneous worship in the grass roots meetings at Moriah Chapel that eventually swept through the nations at the beginning of the 20th century. The emergence of the breakaway culture during the 1960s showcased music that not only came out of a rebellion, but a sound that expressed the cry of a generation with lyrics that spoke to the deeper human condition. The music of the 1960s changed an entire culture. One of my friends and mentors, Julie Anderson, who worked with the Beatles during the height of the '60s puts it this way: "The Church was asleep and still singing yesterday's songs while society ran toward the new sound."

Rick Joyner in his article "The Prophetic Power of Music" says it this way:

> Music is called "the universal language." A communication medium that can cross almost any geographical, ideological or racial barrier, it has a unique ability to touch the soul and arrest the heart. Music is a language of the spirit, and those who know this language and can use it effectively have been entrusted with a potent weapon in the battle for the hearts of this generation…. As we witnessed during the '60s, music can shape the spiritual direction of a generation. The music of the Beatles, and other groups that gained prominence in that decade, both prophesied and sustained the social upheaval of that period…. Artists and musicians often foresee and foretell the social direction of civilization. Similarly, many Christian artists and musicians have the prophetic insight to see the trends and forces shaping the course of the world…. He is anointing prophetic minstrels who will communicate truth that can help set the course for this generation.[6]

Kingdom music has always been released in every generation. Its function? To touch and transform culture. We are called to recognize and make room for the sound being forged and released at this time and in our generation. It is a governing sound, an apostolic sound that carries the spirit of reformation within it. It is a sound that is inhabited with Jesus and His anointing to penetrate the pervading culture of our day, raise spiritual orphans from the dead places of apathy, and provoke the religious to life. The following extract from James Ryle speaks of the new breed of Levites and the distinctive sound they are to carry:

> When I awoke and thought about my dream, I concluded that the Lord was showing me that there was going to be a new and distinctive anointing and sound restored to music that would turn the heads and capture the hearts of men for Jesus Christ. As we stand in the midst of the world and truthfully sing, "In the name of Jesus Christ the Lord we say unto you 'Be Saved!'" This will release the power of His Spirit in such an awesome display that men and women will collapse in their seats and become converted to Christ.
>
> In the dream the Lord showed me that a key to this will be the new anointing He is about to give to His music. What we experienced in the '60s would be nothing compared to what the Lord will do when He releases this new anointing, and He is about to release it again. The Lord showed me clearly that music does not belong to the world; it belongs to the Church. Music was given to worship the Lord but

satan has turned it for self-worship. And now, all around the world, vast crowds of fans tend to worship musicians, and the musicians feed off of this adoration. That is all part of the perversion of the fall.

As my dream concluded, I was holding two photographs in my left hand and a parchment scroll in my right hand. I looked at that scroll and it was a letter written by an unknown soldier of the Salvation Army forty years ago. It was signed "Unknown Soldier." I read this letter and it was a prophecy. It said that the time would come when the Lord God will release into the streets an army of worshipping warriors known as the "Sons of Thunder."[7]

This is an army of apostolic musicians, and the new sound that they carry does not belong to the music industry, Christian or secular. It will not be contained or manufactured, marketed, bought, prostituted, or limited by the constraints of what is profitable, but will be sold out to carrying the government of God within its DNA. Those who partner with it will be committed to carrying the presence of God upon their shoulders and the governing cry of Jesus upon their lips. These musicians, along with the millions of unknowns in the Body of Christ, are being offered the sounds of Heaven to help fulfill the Luke 4:18 mandate—running with what Christ already paid for on the cross to literally see good news heal our sick societies, remove blindness and raise the dead places. As in past generations, this sound has always belonged to Heaven and to the sons of the Kingdom. It is now, more than ever, being discovered again. It deconstructs apathy, cuts through confusion and chaos. It carries Heaven. The question is, *Do we hear it?* Do *you* hear it?

Soundforging Sons of Thunder are being strategically placed for the coming moves of God and are called *to know* and *be known* in the Spirit more than in the natural. Satan, as an influencer in the earth-realm, attempts to release illegitimate passports of promotion to those who will lean into his purpose. As sons and daughters, we are being positioned like Joseph, Daniel, and Esther to engage culture and be used to turn the kingdoms of this world—seeing God's promised redemption of regions and nations. As an entire generation we are being called to be abandoned to the heart of God and known by Heaven long before we are known in the natural. God is releasing legitimate platforms of promotion to Soundforgers all over the nations who will be drafted, short or long term, to hot spots of spiritual breakthrough and spheres of society. They may or may not stand on the platforms of humanity but are moving as unstoppable forces in the hands of God in the hidden war regions of the Spirit.

FORGING SOUND

As a Soundforger, David created instruments for the express purpose of touching Heaven:

> *...four thousand were gatekeepers, and four thousand praised the LORD with musical instruments, "which I made," said David, "for giving praise"* (1 Chronicles 23:5 NKJV).

These instruments expressed harmonies, melodies, and rhythms, forging sound that captured the magnitude of David's own heart for God and also carried and portrayed what he had glimpsed of God's heart toward him and the nations of the Earth. David created instruments to express his own unique contribution to the King's court, releasing within his music what he had heard in Heaven from his times with the Father. David understood the transfer from Heaven to earth in the vehicle of music when his harp melody caused Saul's oppression to lift. (See First Samuel 16:23.) Paul and Silas glimpsed it when prison doors literally broke open as they sang. Israel traded in her trust of weaponry when a shout caused a city to fall and John found himself facedown when he heard the voice that sounded to him like many waters. (See Acts 16:25-27, Joshua 6:20, Revelation 1:12-19.)

At Pentecost, a sound from Heaven was also released over an entire city that drew thousands to encounter God. The speaking of foreign languages could not have been sufficient in itself to draw the multitudes that gathered because Jerusalem was a large multilingual city. Furthermore, this phenomenon also happened during the time of a great feast where even more diverse languages would have been present in the city. We literally see that the wind of God blew across yielded hearts and released a sound that brought an atmospheric shift, causing the blindness that was on the city to be lifted.[8] Those who had previously cried, "Crucify Him!" ran toward the new sound when the Upper Room 120 said yes to the Spirit of God! There is a parallel cry in the Spirit today for musicians to lay down their voices and their sound in order to be a gate for Heaven's sounds and Heaven's voice.

The musicians that I saw in the vision were forging sound with spiritual materials that I did not have a description for. They were endeavoring to receive the resounding heartbeat of Heaven and release it into the Earth. Inhabited and saturated by the Spirit, they were sound-forging according to the heart of God. Just as painters, artists, sculptors, metalworkers, intercessors, or preachers form and forge, so Soundforgers shape with music, sound, melody, and rhythm that which they sense in their spirits, perceive with their minds, feel in the deep, hear with their spiritual ears, see with their spiritual eyes, or sense with their spiritual senses. In this way, they transfer music from God's heart––sound from Heaven to the Earth that carries within it the capacity to release revelatory and governing dimensions.

Forging sound is not a new concept to anyone who has ever experimented with music on any level. Whether standing at the keys of an old piano or touching the skin of a hand drum, the possibilities are countless. The particular parameters or palette of sound that you have to work with determines your voice. When a single inspired voice partners with other voices and is placed within the overall context of a sound that is being formed, music is created. Music can convey, prompt, stir, carry, lead, and project an atmosphere in any arena that it is sounding—a powerful creative force.

The Spirit searches all things, even the deep things of God. For who among men knows the thoughts of a man except the man's spirit within him? In the same way no one knows the thoughts of God except the Spirit of God. We have not received the spirit of the world but the Spirit who is from God, that we may understand what God has freely given us.

This is what we speak, not in words taught us by human wisdom but in words taught by the Spirit, expressing spiritual truths in spiritual words (1 Corinthians 2:10-13).

The deep things of God are made known and expressed in the earth realm through words not taught us by human wisdom but words taught by the Spirit. As Soundforgers, we walk in unfolding understanding of the power of music, sound and songs that receives their origin, motive, and direction from the Holy Spirit. Sons and daughters are indwelt by the Spirit of God and communicated to by Him. He is the One who overhears the conversation of the Father and Son and releases it in the Earth. He is the One who monitors every conversation and heart motive in the earth. He is the One who allows us the capability to receive, interpret, and release Heaven's sound in the Earth; to express the kindness of God or catch aspects of His beauty and authority within our music. As Soundforgers it is crucial that we are anchored in the fundamental truth that the Holy Spirit in us is the only One who can know and reveal the heart of God and inspire the sounds and songs of Heaven. Soundforgers are Heaven carriers and in simple response to God, are literally called to release Heaven's atmosphere wherever they go. One of my favorite Scriptures regarding the activating life that is in us through the Holy Spirit is First John 2:20, "The anointing we've received from Him remains in us and teaches us all things." Jesus also revealed that the Holy Spirit does not speak on His own but only what He *hears* (see John 16:13). He also clearly communicated in language that was from Heaven's dimension and His Father's perspective:

Why is my language not clear to you? Because you are unable to hear what I say. You belong to your father, the devil, and you want to carry out your father's desire. When he (the devil) lies, he speaks his native language, for he is a liar and the father of lies. Yet because I tell the truth, you do not believe me! He who belongs to God hears what God says (John 8:43-45,47).

It is time for music and sound to literally carry the language and communication of Heaven within its DNA. It is time to ask ourselves what righteousness and justice sound like? What sounds express the breaking heart of the Father? What kind of sound accompanies the God of War, the Captain of the Angel Armies as He moves in the Earth? Musicians and vocalists are designed to live abandoned to Heaven and consistently sensitized to recognize certain aspects of the heart and purpose of God and forge sound that is then poured back into the earth. The Father is releasing sensitivity in the arena of revelation upon musicians that is unleashing Spirit-crafted music that brings great corporate breakthrough.

Psalm Drummers, founded by my friend Terl Bryant, is an international grass roots network of drummers who gather together for Kingdom purpose. They put high value upon being sensitized to hearing and responding to the Holy Spirit and musically moving within the heart of God. Sounds of both intimacy and war are forged in drum circles through extended times with God. They are led by the Holy Spirit in corporately crafting incredible sounds that partner with what God is doing in the Earth.

In the coming season, converging with the corporate priestly, prophetic, and apostolic songs, new sounds and styles of music that have not been familiar in church or the world are going to begin to come through God's Soundforgers. They will sense, partner with, and portray God's heart in given moments and concerning given situations. Authoritative sounds and music that have the power to transform, turn sicknesses, and release people from oppressive spirits will be birthed out of a dying to performance and self-promotion—qualities that musicians are trained to esteem. The sounds themselves will not have authority in the Spirit because they are great combinations of musical tone and creativity, but rather will carry authority as they defer to Heaven. The gap is widening between excellently crafted music seeking as an afterthought to be inhabited by Heaven, and Heaven inhabiting a consecrated man or woman and inspiring in them music that He loves. Musicians are being enabled to catch the sounds of Heaven. This is the music that He will put His endorsement and His signature upon in the coming season. God will always honor and bless the things that He sees *Himself* in.

Rick Joyner in his article "The Power of Prophetic Music" states:

> The vision and strategies that the Lord is now giving his Church will be put into songs that will help to seal the hearts of the people with those visions…a powerful anointing that will come from the Heart of the Lord to grip the innermost being of His people. In all of this we must understand that it is not just the sound, but the anointing. The sound is important because the harmony of musical

sound is meant to be concordant with the tone of the message the Holy Spirit is seeking to convey.[9]

Our worship is often restricted by modeling itself after the world's art forms with their sounds, expressions, and melodies. Just as anointed preaching resonates in the Spirit and penetrates, so music is here that carries the mark of the Spirit upon it; music that penetrates the very atmosphere surrounding us.

SOUNDS OF HEAVEN

In looking at priestly, prophetic and apostolic worship we are discovering the interwoven relationship between sound that is offered from earth to Heaven and that which comes from Heaven and is released into the earth. There are dynamic aspects of sound present in Heaven. The fourth chapter of the Book of Revelation gives us insight. John has an incredible encounter with Jesus and seeing an open door into Heaven responds to the invitation. He is exposed to an extended visual encounter and with it the sounds of Heaven:

- ***The Voice of the Father, the Bridegroom, and the Angels***
The voice of the Father and the Bridegroom are heard in Heaven along with declarations and announcements from angelic beings of various kinds. The Father rejoices over us with singing as well as releasing His spoken voice in the earth. What is God singing over your

nation right now? What decrees and declarations are being made by the Creator of the universe? By this Man of War, Counselor, Healer, Lion of Judah?

- ***Songs of Sons and Angels***

The atmosphere of Heaven is permeated with the songs of multitudes of saints from previous generations and of angels and cherubim gathered around the throne of God to worship (see Rev. 5:9).

What is Heaven singing to the Creator right now? What facet of His nature are they worshiping? What songs are the angels releasing over your city and region?

- ***Thunder, Fire, and Water***

Various natural elements are recorded as present in Heaven. Earthquakes, lightning, thunder, rumblings, and fire-blazing lamps all release distinct and powerful sounds (see Rev. 4:5). Jesus' voice is also described as sounding like rushing waters. Fire from the altar is being released from Heaven over the earth. How are you called to partner with it?

- ***Instruments***

The seven trumpets played by angels as the seven seals are opened and the harps played by the 24 elders release sound in Heaven (see Rev. 5:8 and Rev. 8:2). The Lord's voice is also described as *a loud voice like a trumpet*. How are we to forge new combinations of sound as a representation of His voice in the earth?

The spirit of the Moravian prayer movement, the fire of the

Welsh revival and the penetrating prophetic voice of Keith Green are present in Soundforgers right now, in this generation. I encourage you to take hold of the place of connection with the Father and begin to allow the heartbeat and sound of Heaven to resound in you. Whether you discover mercy and tenderness in one moment or justice and war in the next, begin to forge sound and release songs accordingly that will change the atmosphere around your life, the lives of others, and the community and region where you are assigned.

DNA OF THE PSALMS

In the next few chapters we are going to look into the Book of Psalms as the basis for unfolding our understanding of the three strands of priestly, prophetic, and apostolic worship. As the greatest God-song collection ever compiled, many of these crafted verses carry aspects of priestly intimacy, prophetic revelation, and apostolic declaration. Individual Psalms sometimes contain one or all of these dimensions, often changing in focus and direction. Forged within different spiritual climates and seasons, some of these ancient songs are richly personal and others carry a radical outward focus upon the kingdoms and nations of the earth.

God is bringing a progression in the arena of worship that is moving us from the *personal* into the *corporate*. We must grasp this crucial key if we are going to understand and experience what is being released in this season. *Personal* worship is fulfilled in a lifestyle that exists 24/7 in continuous response to our relationship

with Him. However, the full function of corporate worship is not fulfilled simply in a group of separate individuals joining together to
grow in intimacy before the Father—but is to be a setting where *corporate* purpose is realized and God's glory is revealed.

Part of aligning with the current moves of God in praise and
worship is understanding and making provision for various anointings to operate within this expression of corporateness—just as we
see in the Book of Psalms. There is clearly a partnering of both ***intimacy*** and ***war*** as we begin to know and experience the presence
and ways of God in the corporate setting. Isaiah 54:5 speaks to Him
being both our Husband and the Lord of hosts. As we give place to
an increasingly corporate paradigm, aspects of apostolic and
prophetic worship are being released alongside the more familiar
priestly dimension. In previous centuries, pastoral and teaching
content have been evident in praise and worship and are now
accepted as normal in many of our Church settings. Many of our
greatest hymns focus on the eternal truths of God so that we find
ourselves singing doctrine and the truths of our faith. Likewise,
many of our contemporary songs invite us beside the quiet waters
of restoration and intimacy as we sing to the God and Father who
loves us.

Because the global Church has sufficient experiential understanding of the pastoral and teaching aspects within praise and worship, we will not focus on expanding on that further. The attention in
the next few chapters is going to be concentrated on the transition
place we are in currently, and as a starting place, focus in on the
identifiable distinctives of priestly, prophetic, and apostolic worship

that we see modeled in the passages of the Old Testament Psalms.[10] Stay with me as we journey.

ENDNOTES

1. *Strong's New Exhaustive Concordance* (World Bible Publishers, 1980), Hebrew no. 8414 tohuw {to'-hoo}.

2. *Strong's New Exhaustive Concordance* (World Bible Publishers, 1980), Hebrew no. 7363 rachaph {raw-khaf'}.

3. Various research including *Red Moon Rising*, Pete Grieg and Dave Roberts (Relevant Books, 2005), 152.

4. Various research into the Moravians.

5. Florrie Evans, Annie Davies, May John, Kate Morgan, Edith Jones, Mattie Williams & C.A. Jones.

6 Rick Joyner, "The Prophetic Power of Music," *Cross Rhythms Magazine* (Issue 49 Feb/Mar 1999), 63-66.

7. James Ryle, "The Sons of Thunder," *Truthworks*. Used with permission.

8. Bill Johnson, *The Role of the Prophets,* Bethel Church, Redding, CA, August 10, 2006.

9. Rick Joyner, "The Prophetic Power of Music," *Cross Rhythms Magazine* (Issue 49 Feb/Mar 1999), 63-66.

10. Refer to Appendix A for a reference list of priestly, prophetic and apostolic passages from Psalms.

Priestly Worship

Priestly worship operates from earth to Heaven. From the Garden, the Father created a people who would live in unbroken relationship with Him. The priestly dimension is simply the offering of earth to Heaven in love and adoration, expressing the innate desire of man to live in relationship and communication with God. It is the expression of the heart of man given to the heart of God in abandonment. Simply put, we were made for gratitude and made for love. Much of our contemporary praise and worship exists in this priestly dimension. As sons and daughters we were recreated and now live to fulfill our role as priests on the earth. Like contemporary Levites, we live as a captivated people who minister extravagantly, intentionally, and sacrificially to the Father.

The very nature of God and His incredible interaction in our lives calls for response songs in us personally and corporately. We reach up to touch the heart of our Father, grateful for everything that He has done, is doing, and will do. The Spirit of God works in us and is consistently calling out songs from His Bride day and night (see Ps. 65:8). In this way, the Father literally causes righteousness and praise to spring up before all nations as He promised (see Isa. 61:11). Psalm 85 illustrates this well—where faithfulness from the earth and righteousness from Heaven kiss each other. There is a continual cycle of adoration and love from Heaven and response from the earth. Richard Foster says:

> When our reply to God is most direct of all, it is called *adoration*. Adoration is the spontaneous yearning of the heart to worship, honor, magnify, and bless God…in adoration we enter the rarefied air of selfless devotion. We ask for nothing but to cherish him. We seek nothing but his exaltation. We focus on nothing but his goodness…we love God for himself, for his very being, for his radiant joy.[1]

Psalm 30 is an example of an earth-to-Heaven song that remains almost entirely in the priestly dimension and captures the heart of creation's continuous desire to touch Heaven;

> *I will exalt you, O Lord, for you lifted me out of the depths and did not let my enemies gloat over me. O Lord my God, I called to you for help and you healed me. O Lord, you brought me up from the grave; you spared me from going down into the pit…O Lord, when you favored me, you made my mountain stand firm; but when you hid your face, I was dismayed. To you, O Lord, I called; to the Lord I cried for mercy: "What gain is there in my destruction, in my going down into the pit? Will the dust praise you? Will it proclaim*

your faithfulness? Hear, O Lord, and be merciful to me; O Lord, be my help." You turned my wailing into dancing; you removed my sackcloth and clothed me with joy, that my heart may sing to you and not be silent. O Lord my God, I will give you thanks forever (Psalm 30:1-3;7-12).

It speaks consistently to the Father in thanks and abandoned adoration. It celebrates freedom from enemies (see Ps. 30:1), physical healing and protection from death (see Ps. 30:2-3). It speaks of favor and joy (see Ps. 30:5), the response of Heaven in mercy and faithfulness (see Ps. 30:8-10). Weeping gives way to rejoicing and dancing (see Ps. 30:5,11). The psalmist's heart sings and will not be silent (see Ps. 30:12).

UNDERSTANDING PRIESTLY WORSHIP

Priestly psalms speak directly to God and are saturated with thanks—often using the language of intimacy, and express appreciation for the ways and dealings of the Father. They sometimes express desperation to Him, can be sung prayers that call for help on behalf of ourselves or others, and express trust or consecration. Some definite characteristics of this priestly dimension are:

1. ***Priestly*** worship exists in the devotional, continual offering to the Father.
2. It is the drawing near and ***touching the heart*** of God.
3. It is the ***maintenance and release*** of the heartfelt love of the creation for its Creator—connecting earth to

Heaven.

4. It exists to minister to God and bring a blessing to the earth, releasing **mercy on behalf** of those who are not asking for it.

5. **Priestly** worship stands consistently as a **point of faith** in the earth where the Father's heart is open and available to receive us.

Much of our praise and worship experience currently operates in this vital priestly dimension.

BEAUTY REALM

The invitation into relationship with God includes enjoying Him and knowing His beauty—and actually *experiencing* these aspects of His presence. Living in the reality, daily, of how abundant and beautiful He is. Mike Bickle, founder of Friends of the Bridegroom and the International House of Prayer in Kansas City, Missouri, has been a forerunner for the Body in several areas. His personal journey into understanding the place of living before God in His "Beauty Realm" and the insight into the bridal identity of the Church has been invaluable to the Church globally in engaging and enjoying the journey with our Bridegroom Jesus in the priestly dimension of intimacy.

He believes there are several necessary realities that we need as sons and daughters:

1. Walking in a restored confidence in love—being

restored in confidence as a lover of God and assured
we are enjoyed by Him

2. Knowing the Father's tenderness toward us

3. Knowing the affectionate Bridegroom who is full of
    beauty and knowing that we are His Bride and beauti-
    ful to Him

4. Discovering that the Beauty realm is available to us

Bickle also highlights several aspects of our Bridegroom's character that I believe are foundational to the release of priestly worship
in the Earth:[2]

• ***The God of Tenderness***

God delights in showing us lovingkindness. God knows we can
bring nothing to the bargaining table to motivate Him to deal kindly
with us. He is fully motivated within Himself to be merciful.

• ***The God of Gladness***

He smiles with delight and enjoyment when He gazes on each
one of us. This strikes many people as strange. They are accustomed
to relating to a God who is mostly mad or mostly sad when they come
before Him.

• ***The God of Burning Desire***

This fact is deeply rooted in Scripture that He is full of intense
desire and burning love for each of us. He longs to be near each one
of us personally, in the way friends and lovers want to be together.

- ### *The God of Jealous Anger*

The principle underlying jealous anger is this: whatever harms His Bride's preparation as His eternal companion will be judged.

- ### *The God of Fascinating Beauty*

Our Bridegroom possesses a beauty that transcends any other in the created realm. As we encounter it through Scripture and by His revelation in our spirits, His beauty fascinates and captivates our hearts.

At the International House of Prayer they have adopted several models of corporate worship that include: antiphonal singing around apostolic prayers from Scripture, prophetic worship sets, *harp and bowl* worship and intercession. These are the backbone to the fullness and richness of the multifaceted worship dimension that is being released there.

SONSHIP AND A WEDDING

Seeking His face and not His hand is the language of love and the heart behind priestly intimacy. Desiring and dwelling with Him just because He is incredible is the gateway to ongoing relationship with the Father. It is here that we receive insight into knowing God and His heart, which then enables us to partner with Him in the earthly realm. What has been cultivated and treasured in the internal through intimacy will always be the spring from which the Father reveals and propels His life-giving words and sounds that will touch and transform.

Most of our regular corporate gatherings are weighted with moving from the priestly into the pastoral dimension. Out of the earth to Heaven connection, we become aware of the extent of the height, width, and depth of His love. As leaders, from this place in the Spirit we minister to and shepherd individuals and families pastorally. This is a legitimate—but not the only—function of the corporate gathering. The Holy Spirit, out of the place of priestly worship, desires to move us not only into the pastoral but into the revelatory and governing dimensions of prophetic and apostolic purpose.

In the last 50 years the priestly dimension has emerged in songs that speak directly to the Father using words that express intimacy and adoration. We have moved out of singing only hymns that are about God or reinforce aspects of doctrine, and toward engaging our hearts and experiencing Him, communicating directly to Him how we truly feel about a God of untamable, unfathomable love.

> *Therefore I am now going to allure her; I will lead her into the desert and speak tenderly to her. There I will give her back her vineyards, and will make the Valley of Achor (trouble) a door of hope...."In that day," declares the Lord, you will call me 'my husband'; you will no longer call me 'my master'* (Hosea 2:14-16).

In places of priestly worship, He draws us, speaks tenderly, and offers hope to us in new dimensions. Slavery gives way to sonship. Friendship gives way to a wedding.

I will betroth you to me forever; I will betroth you in right-eousness and justice, in love and compassion. I will betroth you in faithfulness, and you will acknowledge the Lord (Hosea 2:19-20).

Throughout all generations, we have been captivated by the tender, merciful, loving, and forgiving Creator who so desires to be with us that He initiated the restoration of relationship through the blood of His own Son. We are loved and learn to love in increasing dimensions as the journey of the relationship unfolds. Out of this place of intimacy, the Father acts and speaks tenderly, anchoring us in love, identity and security.

As Soundforgers minister, willing as a nameless and faceless priesthood, those they lead are given new names of empowerment and worth in the presence of God. Face to face with the Father, they receive an imprint of adoption that transforms their DNA and propels them to walk in Heaven's intended identity. A facedown generation is here, prepared to lay down lives and destinies for the sake of know-ing Him more. They are accessing places of limitless intimacy with God. Abandoned to Him, as they wait long enough to listen, they receive their true identity and purpose. They do not lament over never receiving their lives back—because dead is dead—and the life being offered is not comparable with what was lived before. To this breed of seekers only one thing is required. Only one thing is needed. Only One person satisfies.

Married to the One, Soundforgers are responding to the continu-ous invitation from Heaven and are forging songs of extravagant expression and devotion that touch the heart of the Father as an offering from the earth. Many musicians and worship leaders have been captivated by their Bridegroom. They now walk in a lifestyle of worship that truly causes them to operate as a priest in the earth realm. This is the only starting place for us—relationship, being, and intimacy.

The priestly dimension in worship is the ultimate place of personal expression to God.

ENDNOTES

1. Richard J. Foster, *Prayer: Finding the Heart's True Home* (San Francisco, CA: HarperSanFrancisco, 1992), 81.

2. Mike Bickle, *After God's Own Heart* (Lake Mary, FL: Charisma House, 2004), 33-41.

C h a p t e r   4

Prophetic Worship

As God has restored prophets and prophetic operation to the Church, we have become more familiar with distinct areas of prophetic function. Activation as individuals in hearing His voice, personal prophecy, prophetic intercession, the seer dimension of dreams and visions,[1] and prophetic preaching are all recognizable and acceptable areas of prophetic activity.

There are many incredible books[2] that speak into this but in searching Scripture we can basically divide prophetic operation this way:

- A spirit of prophecy (see 1 Sam. 10:9-12)—the release of the Holy Spirit upon an individual or a group that causes an activation of revelation and the release of the prophetic that does not normally operate. Saul's encounter with the prophets in First Samuel 10:9-12 highlights an unexpected experience. The spirit of prophecy activated Saul, who actually stood in the office of a king, into prophesying night and day.

- General prophecy (see Acts 2:17-19)—all should prophesy and communicate the heart and mind of God to those around them.

- Gift of prophecy (see 1 Cor. 12:10b, 1 Cor.14:29, Acts 21:9)—a resident gift of prophecy, accuracy in revelation, an approach to life through a prophetic lens but not standing in the office of a prophet.

- Office of a prophet (see Eph. 4:11, Acts 13:1)—A functioning governmental individual recognized by, submitted to, and functioning in a single or in multiple local churches, carrying enlarged kingdom influence and equipping the Body of Christ in the prophetic dimension alongside apostles and the other five-fold offices.

- Prophecy of Scripture—no longer being added to because Scripture is complete.

Wherever we currently operate in the prophetic dimension, we can intentionally position ourselves to expand within the call of God. As individuals within local Churches, healthily submitted to leadership, we must believe in and be equipped for an increase in the prophetic and in our ability to hear, perceive and communicate accurately. Jesus said only what He heard His Father saying and the Spirit who lives in us does not speak on His own but only what He hears (see

John 5:30, John 14:26). This is incredible because we are inhabited by and live in intimacy with a Person whose job description is to lead us into all truth and speak to us only what he hears from Heaven. We are, out of this relationship, taught words to speak to individuals, families, churches, cities, regions, states, and nations (1 Cor. 2:10). We are connected to the One who speaks and is not silent, and according to Isaiah 30:30, causes men to hear His voice. Amos spoke of a time when there would be a famine of the Word of the Lord, when there would be fainting and wandering through an absence of the prophetic word. Many of us have been in seasons where revelation seemingly dried up—but our sons and daughters are prophesying (see Acts 2:17) and the prophets are being recognized and restored in the land.

To understand God's agenda for prophetic worship, we must be aware that we are currently experiencing a shift where prophetic insight beyond the individual level is being released in our corporate gatherings. Prophets and prophetic people are moving beyond the borders of simply sharing Heaven's heart and mind for individuals to revealing strategy and direction for the corporate. Previously, in many settings, the platform provided for prophetic ministry has been limited to releasing personal words to individuals—giving instruction or revelation for the edification, comfort, or exhortation of that person (see 1 Cor. 14:3). This is a legitimate expression of the prophetic dimension, but not a place to stop, remain and set up a monument. There is a wider mode of operation designated by God to His prophets and prophetic people. They are designed to bring revelation that enables our corporate gatherings to complete all they are called to accomplish.

There is a definite maturing taking place in our understanding of the place and function of the prophetic in the 21st-century Church. In the corporate setting we are navigating through the blending of the five-fold functions and anointings for increased purpose and greater Kingdom advancement. The prophetic dimension, among other things, releases vision, describes the new places in God seen through the eyes of the Spirit, provides insight into happenings in the realm of the Spirit, charges the Church with specific assignments, and speaks alignment, enlargement, and hope to our future. We are not called to be disoriented but to clearly understand the corporate season. The prophetic dimension provides revelation as to where the Church is moving, and helps us secure accurate timing and define precise action regarding Heaven's plan when we gather.

We are heading for exciting times as we embrace the full function of prophets and prophetic people into the Church and simply move from a *me* mentality to a *we* paradigm. The prophetic function will release us into a dimension where we are corporately sensitized to perceive the moment—the "now" of God—from Heaven's perspective. Our corporate gatherings will become charged with supernatural life as the inclusion of true and tested prophetic ministry is folded into the corporate flow of our gatherings. Precise alignment with the agenda of Heaven in every setting—be it moments or entire spiritual seasons—will become more and more acceptable to us as we gather corporately.

THE PROPHETIC IN WORSHIP

Music and the prophetic have had a longstanding history in

Scripture, not only in relation to the Tabernacle of David, which appointed men of musical status who *prophesied* on their instruments, but also in an apparent thread that illustrates the prophetic and worship working together.

In preparation to prophesy to a group of kings, Elisha the prophet calls for a minstrel to play (see 2 Kings 3:14-20). The company of prophets who meet Saul coming down from the high places operate alongside musicians (see 1 Sam. 10:5). Moses (see Exod. 15:1) and Deborah (see Judg. 5:1) sing spontaneous songs that emerge from their circumstances, and Miriam takes a portion of Moses' song and leads the people with it. New songs are also featured in Heaven (see Rev. 5:9), and now in the New Covenant, we are urged to eagerly desire to prophesy (see 1 Cor.14:1). As Soundforgers, we do this by speaking and singing prophetically to each other, our cities, communities, governments, and the lost in our nation.

Just as we identified Psalms that operate primarily in the priestly dimension so there are specific Psalms that are primarily prophetic—carrying revelatory content that focuses upon communicating the heart and mind of God.

PROPHETIC PSALMS

Psalm 128 carries several dimensions of the prophetic:

Blessed are all who fear the Lord, who walk in his ways. You will eat the fruit of your labor; blessings and prosperity will be yours. Your wife will be like a fruitful vine within your

house; your sons will be like olive shoots around your table.
Thus is the man blessed who fears the Lord. May the Lord
bless you from Zion all the days of your life; may you see the
prosperity of Jerusalem, and may you live to see your chil-
dren's children. Peace be upon Israel (Psalm 128:1-6).

The Father speaks through the psalmist regarding the blessing
that rests on us when we walk with Him. God's favor is promised in
the workplace and the home, and over husbands, wives, and children. An extended life of blessing and the prosperity of our cities
along with peace upon our nation are prophesied. What a great
prophetic word of blessing!

Psalm 22 is Messianic-prophetic and depicts the crucifixion of
Jesus centuries before He walked the earth, and long before this form
of the death penalty existed. It is amazing that through worship, God
revealed the plan of salvation to a Soundforger.[3]

My God, my god, why have you forsaken me?…a band of evil
men has encircled me, they have pierced my hands and my
feet. They divide my garments among them and cast lots for
my clothing…. They will proclaim his righteousness to a peo-
ple yet unborn—for he has done it (Psalm 22:1,16,18,31).

Prophetic psalms then, speak from God to man—expressing
communication from Him to a specific audience. Communication
targets can include: His people, His enemies, specific cities, regions,
and people groups; the revealing of God's eternal or current intent

in specific situations; the release of revelation, understanding and wisdom.

THE PROPHETIC DIMENSION IN WORSHIP

The prophetic dimension in worship functions in various ways and carries certain characteristics:

1. Prophetic worship evolves from priestly relationship and *unlocks understanding* from Heaven into the earth.

2. Prophetic revelation is released in *many different forms*: communication from a prophet, a Rhema[4] word from Scripture, a vision or picture, a sensing of direction, a section of an already written song that becomes infused with present-moment revelation, a spontaneous prophetic song, the predetermined focus of the gathering by leaders.

3. Prophetic worship reveals the heart and mind of God releasing Heaven's perspective. Dividing truth from error, it *calls this realm to recognize the way things are* from a Heavenly perspective. It is the function of the necessary and needed revelation from the Creator to His creation.

4. *Prophetic revelation in worship raises and reinstates Heaven's reality* as a relevant plumb line in the earth. More than an offering from earth to Heaven, the prophetic brings God's mind and

thoughts on circumstances which displaces all other perceived truth and understanding. Partnered with the written Word of God, this is a powerful force to bring change.

CHARACTERISTICS OF PROPHETIC WORSHIP

In a musical context, prophetic worship:

- Searches for the ***mind and perspective*** of Heaven regarding those being led in worship, an individual, a Church, a geographic region, a government, or nation.

- ***Harvests the headlines*** and translates this under-standing from the heart of God into a musical or vocal form. Its *content* can include Scripture with a "now" focus or contain spontaneous words.

- Will almost always move in ***edification, comfort, and exhortation*** (see 1 Cor. 14:3).

- Causes an ***alignment with the heart and mind of God*** which can prepare for and prompt a change in direction or focus resulting in a corporate response or action.

- When sung corporately, prophetic songs bring people

together in one mind and focus, shifting us into **higher realms** of corporate purpose.

- Allows a continued "**maneuvering** within the heart of God" to a place where there is a flow of revelation being received and we are sensitized to the "now," (or *kairos*) of God.

- **Types of prophetic song and music** include: communicating revelation, instruction and wisdom songs, encouragement, exhortation and comfort, healing songs from the Father's heart, and instrumental music that activates the prophetic.

PROPHETIC SOUNDFORGERS

Soundforgers are emerging with varying degrees of prophetic calling and operation within their ministry function. Some are moved by a spirit of prophecy when the Holy Spirit falls and those who do not normally prophesy or are not normally recognized as having a residential gift of prophecy begin to move much more clearly and strongly in the arena of revelation. When first leading worship as a new believer, the sense of God using my musical gifting and operating through my life prophetically would be enlarged when I partnered with other ministries that were much more seasoned in the prophetic and full of Heaven's delegated authority. I found myself operating in dimensions of the Spirit that were not normally resident, but which simply functioned for a purpose in that setting. Some Soundforgers are emerging as prophetic voices to their generation within specific spheres of influence. They experience a consistent resident operation of the prophetic within their music and are used as corporate prophetic catalysts in worship settings.

I have been fortunate to lead several mentoring groups to unlock prophetic vocalists. They have usually functioned as grassroots gatherings of opportunity to encounter the prophetic anointing and understand how it teaches us (see 1 John 2:20). I have discovered that some individual musicians and vocalists operate in the prophetic mainly through sensing impressions from the heart of God, and others see pictures or visions. Some hear direct prophetic words and sing them out, while certain people are drawn to a *rhema* word from Scripture. Becoming increasingly sensitized to the changes in intensity of the presence and heart of God enables them to determine the appropriateness of timing in releasing a particular thought or idea. Training sessions combine activating prophetic, spontaneous songs and pausing to discuss what was sensed, perceived, or experienced. Corporate unity invites cohesive revelation that becomes a big picture for understanding what God is ultimately saying.

Just as the prophets under the Old Covenant spoke messages, told parables, used symbolism, and performed prophetic acts, so New Testament prophecy[5] is released in countless culturally relevant forms. Just as the men of Issachar understood the times (see 1 Chron. 12:32) and Jesus Himself lived a lifestyle communicating incredible reality parables, so Soundforgers are called to carry the prophetic language of today's and tomorrow's dimension. It is crucial for us to move in new levels of creativity that touch a generation. The secular media is prophesying its agenda to our children and youth. We must respond violently to the wake-up call being issued to the Church to understand God's heart for our generation. The time is now for us to begin to prophesy for the four winds to come into dry and dead places. The breath of God is moving through the prophetic to awaken dry bones with revelation. Call for an army to be pieced together and rise with the specific strategy engulfed by the power of God!

Throughout Scripture many prophetic words were delivered to individuals and people groups, but the prophetic Psalms mentioned previously are placed in the form of songs that were sung as part of Israel's praise and worship experience and originally crafted by the Davidic Levites in the Tabernacle. In addition to the functions already mentioned, they stand to remind the Lord of His acts and His Word (see Ps. 77:11), release revelation (see Ps. 22), engage prophetic intercession (see Ps. 72:1-5) or are sung out in the Spirit as a declaration (see Ps. 46:1-8). This is a *legitimate Kingdom model for us today* as we understand the unfolding of prophetic worship.

Where anointings are released to freely function, places in corporate worship are being released that are literally propelling whole groups of people—whether 50 or 5,000—to release new songs that are to be priestly, prophetic, or apostolic in nature.

THE *NOW* OF GOD

Perceiving and communicating the *now* of God is one function of the prophetic and a key to activating the corporate gathering in new dimensions of purpose and authority. By the *now* of God, I simply mean, the sensitization and perception of what He is doing right now, in the moment—rather than what He *did* do, or *will* do at sometime in the future. Some of our meetings naturally have a devotional focus, and others target strategy or have an outward evangelistic focus. Whatever the purpose, the Holy Spirit is always waiting to communicate Heaven's Word for the moment. Whether we are teaching timeless foundational principles of forgiveness, discovering how the early Church walked throughout the Book of Acts, hearing a prophetic word for an individual or a nation, or declaring a shift across an entire geographic region, the Holy Spirit is working to make the heart of the Father known, relevant, and able to be grasped and appropriated.

I require my worship teams to lend themselves and be sensitized to the *now* of God in every worship setting. It is crucial for the current *mark* of God to be present in the corporate. I personally believe that the level of syncing with the *now* of God is directly proportional to the level of power and the miraculous that is released. This is why the prophetic dimension is so important in every aspect of Body ministry and especially worship.

EMBRACING PROPHETIC WORSHIP

Corporate prophetic worship has often been held at arm's length simply because it often differs from the priestly love offering of earth to Heaven. It does not in any way *negate* or *replace* what Churches or gatherings have been comfortable with doing, but works alongside

as another facet of the corporate function in the hand of a multifaceted God.

If we take a look at a cross section of biblical worship, the focus
varies and moves between petition, adoration, intimacy, declaration,
and in the *Old* Testament, even vengeance (see Ps. 68:1-3).

Prophetic worship is still Father-centered like the priestly but
includes a dimension of being in the "now" of the Spirit-led that causes
it to be pregnant with revelation. Out of the place of intimacy we
search for and hear what the Father is speaking, catching the perspective of Heaven for such areas as a geographic region, a government or
an individual, then release it musically and vocally. Prophetic worship
assumes that the Father releasing revelation in the corporate is both
acceptable and necessary. These prophetic songs when sung corporately bring the body together into unity around what the Holy Spirit is
specifically communicating in that setting. This shifts us into higher
realms of corporate purpose. Prophetic worship releases and lays out
revelation which can be harvested for accurate corporate purpose and
declaration. Prophetic worship urges alignment with the mind and
heart of God and can prepare the corporate for governing declarations
that may be made by apostles and prophets that cause a shift to occur.

> *Where priestly worship is the ultimate place of personal*
> *expression, prophetic worship is the hinge-pin in moving*
> *into the place of receiving revelation of what is on the*
> *heart and mind of God.*

ENDNOTES

1. James W. Goll, *The Seer* (Shippensburg, PA: Destiny Image, 2004). This is the most current and informative book available on the distinction between the visual *seer* prophets and verbal *nabi* prophets.

2. Please see Appendix C for a list of suggested books.

3. Concept taken from conversation with a friend, Alan Coulter, Nashville, TN, January 2007.

4. A *rhema* word (Strong's Greek no. 4487) is defined as a *now* word from Heaven that becomes highlighted to us from within Scripture—the *logos* word. A rhema word, like a prophetic marker, brings direction or understanding to a particular situation or season from Heaven's perspective. Jesus said in Matthew 4:4, "Man does not live on bread alone, but on every word (*rhema*) that comes from the mouth of God."

5. God is currently bringing clarity to the function of the Five-fold ministry. One subject being highlighted for Prophets and Prophetic people is the need to distinguish between the role and function of prophesy in the Old Covenant compared to the New. Since the Cross and Resurrection we are now living in a different dispensation—where prophesy does not operate today like it did in the Old Testament. Please refer to the list of suggested books for expansion on this subject.

Government

Having looked at aspects of earth to Heaven priestly worship and revelatory prophetic worship, we want to now focus in on the government of God, the apostolic, and the concept of making decrees and declarations. Before we move into apostolic worship we need to establish a foundation that will enable us to gain context for much of what is being released. In order to move in greater realms of authority, Soundforgers must be aligned with a correct biblical view of authority and God's government. It is important that we solidify these key concepts before moving into the different dimensions that God is restoring in worship. Stay with me as we move through this chapter—it is going to be crucial in understanding what is coming next.

THE REALM OF CHRIST'S GOVERNMENT

Even though our primary identity as individual believers is as a son or daughter, functionally we are not able to separate ourselves from God's corporate government. We are simultaneously both a family and a Kingdom. The Church represents God's Kingdom and therefore His government on the earth, and its governmental leaders stand as His Generals in the operational realm. We have been gaining understanding of the five-fold ministry—apostles, prophets, pastors, teachers, and evangelists. God is giving us accelerated revelation of how these people-gifts engage together with the Body of Christ for Kingdom advancement. Each one differs in function within this Kingdom, carrying distinct gifts and spheres of operation. Ephesians 4:11 introduces the offices to us:

> It was he [Jesus] who gave some to be apostles, some to be prophets, some to be evangelists, and some to be pastors and teachers, to prepare God's people for works of service, so that the body of Christ may be built up until we all reach unity in the faith and in the knowledge of the Son of God and become mature, attaining to the whole measure of the fullness of Christ (Ephesians 4:11-13).

The primary function of these governmental leaders is to equip the Body for the work of ministry, facilitating unity and a maturing process so that the fullness of Christ can be experienced in the earth. Alone, they bring focus to one facet of who Christ is. Together they require the fullness of Christ be seen in the earth and His complete purpose released. Among these, the function of the apostle and the apostolic dimension has been the least understood and the most debated, but nevertheless it remains a crucial function within the unfolding of God's government for a variety of reasons. I do not want to debate the specific issues surrounding the entitling, abuse, and misuse of people operating as apostles today; however, I am convinced that the *function* of the office is paramount to the future of the Church and most importantly, societal transformation. It is important to realize that five-fold leaders and particularly apostles are emerging in every one of the primary spheres of society. Apostles in the realm of media, government, education, arts and entertainment, family, and business are being recognized and positioned along with those who are called to function as apostles in the Church. The apostolic anointing is crucial to our walk in all we are called to. Jesus intentionally chose to use a common military term rather than a religious one when referring to his disciples as *apostles*. Typically, this role encompassed enforcing the new ruler's kingdom upon a recently captured city or region. The apostolic function transitioned the occupants into living by the rules of a new order. Apostles were by nature delegated, *sent* enforcers.

Several leaders have the following to say about this office today:

- Peter Wagner states; "An apostle is a Christian leader, gifted, taught, commissioned, and sent by God with authority to establish the foundational government of the Church within an assigned sphere of ministry by hearing what the Spirit is saying to the Churches and by setting things in order accordingly for the growth and maturity of the Church." [1]

- Kris Vallotton defines an Apostle as someone who carries a mission from Heaven that people come into submission to and get commissioned. [2]

- Barbara Yoder, focusing upon the early Church, says, "If we were to study the book of Acts to decipher the function or mandate of apostles, we would see that apostles govern; exercise territorial authority (by breaking into new, previously unevangelized geographical territories); reproduce or multiply themselves; build and establish the Church; finish or complete what they have started, and send out believers to accomplish Kingdom purposes...The Church in America, through a nonbiblical paradigm, has evolved into a people who are onlookers and bystanders...with the restoration of the apostolic church, a new force is rising."[3]

- John Eckhardt clearly identifies the early Church as an apostolic Church under the authority of apostles. "The Church in the book of Acts was first and foremost an apostolic Church. They understood they were sent ones. They knew they were authorized to carry out this mission. The dominant anointing in the book of Acts was apostolic...the apostolic set the tone for the early church; it moulded who they were and what they did."[4]

- Dr. Paula Price affirms that, "understanding apostleship always hinges upon two immutable things: gods and nations."[5]

Paul often speaks openly about the reality of walking out his call as an apostle. This passage in Second Corinthians speaks more about the heart and endurance of the office of an apostle than the function.

> *We put no stumbling block in anyone's path, so that our ministry will not be discredited. Rather, as servants of God we commend ourselves in every way: in great endurance; in troubles, hardships and distresses; in beatings, imprisonments and riots; in hard work, sleepless nights and hunger; in purity, understanding, patience and kindness; in the Holy Spirit and in sincere love; in truthful speech and in the power of God; with weapons of righteousness in the right hand and in the left; through glory and dishonor, bad report and good report; genuine, yet regarded as impostors; known, yet regarded as unknown; dying, and yet we live on; beaten, and yet not killed; sorrowful, yet always rejoicing; poor, yet making many rich; having nothing, and yet possessing everything* (2 Corinthians 6:3-10).

These are incredible, death-to-self responses from a man who had regularly seen the power of God in miracles, signs, and wonders. Called as an apostle, referred to as a friend, a servant to nations, Paul was simply called to live for something bigger than a title or a ministry, something greater than himself. I believe that the blending of these two paradigms—the apostle as both a sent enforcer of the Kingdom and a Servant friend gives us a foundational glimpse of who the apostle is. Today, because apostles are emerging in every sphere of society, we must have clear understanding of their function and character. We must also move in apostolic anointing as individual believers and see that our corporate role as the apostolic Church is grasped and operational. These definitions of an apostle can help us understand apostolic worship and anointings and give us clarity as to what the apostolic church under the leadership of five-fold government is to look like.

THE KINGDOM AND ITS MANDATES

Jesus taught and *demonstrated* the Kingdom of God throughout His assignment here on the earth. The word *king-dom* literally refers to the domain of a king—the king's domain. God's Kingdom is clearly shown by Jesus to be superior to every other kingdom. We see the sick and demonized freed, and personally experience a love that is so strong that it chose to give up life to buy us back—conquering sin, death and hell forever. This is the nature of His Kingdom! Experiencing the increasing and overcoming domain of this King of tenacious love is a key to seeing fullness in the realm of worship. Jesus spoke many parables about the Kingdom, revealing that it is *here,* and it is *within* us:

> *Heal the sick who are there and tell them, "The kingdom of God is near you"* (Luke 10:9).

> *Once, having been asked by the Pharisees when the kingdom of God would come, Jesus replied, "The kingdom of God does not come with your careful observation, nor will*

people say, 'Here it is,' or 'There it is,' because the kingdom of
God is within you (Luke 17:20-21).

Along with emerging as an apostolic people, we are clearly in a season where the demonstration of the Kingdom, not just education about salvation, is breaking out. Just like the early Church, this requires us to lock into Kingdom mandates like never before. Three foundational mandates that have been released to us as the Church are:

a) ***The Creation Mandate***—Genesis 1:26-28

Then God said, "Let us make man in our image, in our likeness,
and let them rule over the fish of the sea and the birds of the
air, over the livestock, over all the earth, and over all the crea-
tures that move along the ground." So God created man in his
own image, in the image of God he created him; male and
female he created them. God blessed them and said to them,
"Be fruitful and increase in number; fill the Earth and subdue it.
Rule over the fish of the sea and the birds of the air and over
every living creature that moves on the ground."

b) ***Jesus' Mission Statement***—Luke 4:18-19

"The Spirit of the Lord is on me, because he has anointed me to
preach good news to the poor. He has sent me to proclaim
freedom for the prisoners and recovery of sight for the blind, to
release the oppressed, to proclaim the year of the Lord's favor."

c) ***The Great Commission***—Mark 16:15-19

"Go into all the world and preach the good news to all cre-
ation. Whoever believes and is baptized will be saved, but
whoever does not believe will be condemned. And these
signs will accompany those who believe: In my name they
will drive out demons; they will speak in new tongues; they
will pick up snakes with their hands; and when they drink
deadly poison, it will not hurt them at all; they will place
their hands on sick people, and they will get well."

Sojourn Church in Dallas, Texas, our apostolic base, has used
Luke 4:18 as its mandate for the last two decades. The Old Testament mirror-passage in Isaiah 61 speaks of a people who will
rebuild ancient ruins and restore places long devastated. This is
speaking of an activated Kingdom—demonstration people—the
apostolic Church. Each one of these mandates requires the corporate Church and individuals to look beyond themselves and
advance the Kingdom of God in every sphere they touch, to literally
live operating within an apostolic paradigm. Most lead worshipers
are content to remain in the pastoral or priestly mindset, functioning from earth to Heaven—with a shepherding emphasis. If we
remain here and do not grasp the outward focus of the Kingdom
mandates given to the Church and work with new aspects of what
the Holy Spirit is releasing, we may not be enabled to partner with
seeing the corporate Body shift into the fullness that God intends.
A sure grasp of God's mandates and the governmental realm is a

crucial key in order to step into what God is releasing in worship, in each sphere of society and in our corporate gatherings. Just looking deeply into the cry of your own heart, you will discover that there is a river in you that wants to flow out. There is a son in you who is created to inherit, and there is a kingly dimension that is intended to rule!

As we attempt to infuse these Kingdom mandates into society, Dutch Sheets in *Authority in Prayer* gives us valuable foundational insight. He relays four reasons why it is critical for us to begin living with a foundation of believing that Christ has dominion and is the ultimate authority of all:[6]

1. Only those who have authority can delegate it. If Christ doesn't have complete dominion over the Earth, He can't give it to us.

2. Understanding Christ's ownership and authority over all the Earth brings great faith to fulfill our callings and assignments, including, of course, our personal world.

3. Without Christ's true ownership of and authority over the Earth, the final outcome of this battle for Earth could be in doubt.

4. We must submit to Christ's authority before He will delegate His authority to us.

In the natural dimension we are called as the Church to submit to the Government of God and engage with the earthly governmental structures of man. However, we can become so familiar with operating in the natural arena in terms of legal petitions, lobbying, and campaigning that we can find ourselves inactive in moving with God's mandates in the realm of the Spirit where God's judicial system and rule ultimately exist and operate. Dutch Sheets clearly defines the role of the Church in spiritual legislation:

> When Jesus used the word Church (Greek: ekklesia), the disciples weren't hindered by our contemporary preconceived ideas as to what it meant. Their paradigm of an ekklesia differed greatly from what it has become....To the Greeks in Christ's day an ekklesia was an assembly of people set apart to govern the affairs of a state or nation—in essence, a parliament or congress. To the Romans, it was a group of people sent to conquer a region to alter the culture until it became like Rome. Realizing this was the ideal way to control their empire, they infiltrated government, social structure, language, schools etc., until the people talked, thought and acted like Romans. When Jesus said He would build His Church, He was without question speaking of a body of people that would legislate spiritually for Him, extending His Kingdom government (rule) over the Earth.[7]

The Ancient of Days has always ruled, and through His creation mandate in the garden released the commission for man to have dominion. Jesus sealed this forever and is now seated at the right hand of the Father, with *all* things under Him—and with *all* authority in Heaven and earth being given to Him (see Eph. 1:20-23; Matt. 28:18). This has incredible ramifications for Soundforgers who are called to transmit His sound and declarations from Heaven. Sound-forgers must understand their role in legislation as they unite with the court of Heaven to lead the corporate Body in the days ahead. Cindy Jacobs, cofounder of Generals International, is a prophet who has incredible anointing in the realm of governmental declaration and legislation. She teaches on, and engages the court of Heaven for the unlocking of hinge places in regions and nations. I have had the privilege of working alongside Cindy many times in settings where God released powerful prophetic and apostolic anointings, and worship in corporate gatherings.

We know that righteousness and justice are the foundation of the throne of God. Today, the Court of Heaven is functioning over our nations legislating the rule and reign of God. In a night vision, Daniel releases incredible revelation of the court of Heaven and of the One who sits and convenes.

> As I looked, thrones were set in place, and the Ancient of Days took His seat. His clothing was as white as snow; the hair of His head was white like wool. His throne was flaming with fire, and its wheels were all ablaze. A river of fire was flowing, coming out from before Him. Thousands upon thousands attended Him; ten thousand times ten thousand stood before Him. The court was seated, and the books were opened (Daniel 7:9-11).

In my vision at night I looked, and there before me was one like a Son of man, coming with the clouds of heaven. He approached the Ancient of Days and was led into His presence. He was given authority, glory and sovereign power; all peoples, nations and men of every language worshiped Him. His dominion is an everlasting dominion that will not pass away, and His Kingdom is one that will never be destroyed.... As I watched, this horn was waging war against the saints and defeating them until the Ancient of Days came and pronounced judgment in favor of the saints of the Most High, and the time came when they possessed the kingdom (Daniel 7:13-14;21-22).

We are living in a place of fulfilling Heaven's mandates where Jesus clearly has been crowned King and where the court of Heaven convenes to release Heaven's justice into earthly governments. Through the death and resurrection of Christ, The Ancient of Days has pronounced judgment in favor of His saints, and He has assigned us to *possess and enforce* this Kingdom of righteousness and justice. We are living in a day where the court is in session over our nations. The verdict has been issued to those who are in Christ, and the Government of God has been released to His sent ones—the apostolic Church—and to His apostolic Soundforgers.

SPHERES OF AUTHORITY

New levels of Kingdom purpose are requiring us to understand spheres of authority in a new way, especially as we see the release of prophetic and apostolic worship in new dimensions. Our sphere of authority can be understood by several factors:

- Our God-given call and designated realm of operation.

- The evidence of sufficient power, grace, and the life of God functioning to fulfill the mandate or call.

- Clear recognition by our leaders and peers.

Spheres of authority are not limited to individuals but are set for all organizations and organisms. Businesses have their designated position of influence, and a local church in a specific location will operate in the realm of authority designated to them by God. For example, it may have regional recognition in a specific arena of ministry, host conferences that gather the Body, or function with apostolic teams that feed into the life of other local churches.

The early Church apostles clearly understood their specific realm of jurisdiction and boundaries set by the Holy Spirit in their ministry function (see 2 Cor. 10:13-17). Even though each one of them operated under the jurisdiction of the Kingdom and the Great Commission, specific mandates were clarified by God to them personally. Peter received a mandate to go to the Gentiles in a vision (see Acts 10:9), but this was not the call of every early Church apostle. Paul and Barnabus were sent by the Church in Jerusalem for the assignment God had given them—which resulted in the birth of the Apostolic

Church and sending base in Antioch. Paul is also clear about those he had authority over—stating that His apostleship clearly extended to the Corinthian Church (see 2 Cor. 10:13). It also is clear that certain churches and regions were closed to him at specific times by the Spirit (see Acts 16:6-7). Today, apostles also have a clear measure of authority and boundaries within their call and function. In the Church realm, they can be simply identified as either *vertical*—presiding over networks or churches, or *horizontal* as they gather peer level leaders. [8] Apostles, prophets, pastors, evangelists, and teachers predominantly operating in the local church have a given sphere of oversight over those they equip. Marketplace apostles are marked with God's authority within their sphere of expertise to bring breakthrough and advancement in their field. As leaders, they are also responsible for those employees whom they lead and serve. Spheres of authority are clearly defined in every arena of life. Police officers have specific jurisdiction in their roles as law enforcers. A principal of a particular *high school* does not have influence on a governmental level over the *elementary school* that her son attends. She can offer advice and experience, suggesting alternative ways to help the school function, but does not carry jurisdictional authority to implement or make decisions. I am currently the pastor overseeing worship at my home church but do not have automatic authority in another regional church without being invited or given authority. I am simply not a pastor there! These are simple examples highlighting a principle that must be grasped as we move forward to operate in the realm of the Spirit.

Jesus operated in the sphere of influence given to Him and lived in response and complete submission to Heaven's voice:

> I do nothing on my own authority, but speak just as the
> Father taught me (John 8:28 ESV).

> I tell you the truth, the Son can do nothing by himself; he can
> do only what he sees his Father doing, because whatever the
> Father does the Son also does (John 5:19).

As we hear His voice and become saturated with Heaven's man-dates, we are ultimately propelled forward into alignment to see Heaven on earth in greater dimensions. We are invited to live in increased revelation as to what is on God's heart, partnered with the infiltration of the power and authority to accomplish what He is revealing. In our corporate gatherings, Soundforgers are being acti-vated to operate in arenas in the Kingdom that they have not been used to. As this happens we must understand that our sphere of authority is not an independent sphere and is actually somewhat determined by those we are in submission to or in relationship with. In partnering with an apostle, prophet, or another five-fold leader in a specific Kingdom purpose we often experience a measure of that person's gifting implemented through our ministry, basically experi-encing authority by association.[9] A great example in the Old Testa-ment is the well-known story of the battle with the Amalekites in Exodus 17:8-15. Joshua was being prepared to be Israel's leader but only had victory when Moses' arms were raised. We can always tell when we are working under someone else's mantle because whenever they lower their arms, we begin to lose....[10]

We must understand that our sphere of influence in a particular setting is directly tied to the sphere of authority of the leader or leaders who are responsible in that setting. Until we are recognized by a local church or larger sector of the global Church and *released into* a greater sphere of authority, we should seek to operate within our current sphere of influence or under authority by association. This requires adequate relationship, accountability, and clear communication. Understanding that we must be *under* authority to *have* authority is a foundation stone that Jesus was trying to help us understand when He mentioned that those that desire to be great in the Kingdom had to be servants to everyone (see 1 Pet. 5:6). It is also encouraging to know that as we humble ourselves before God, promotion comes to us at the right time and season (see Matt. 20:26). Active humility and understanding servant leadership are keys of revelation to being promoted to greater levels of authority.

We can sometimes find ourselves having been anointed by God but not yet anointed by man or the other way around.[11] The bottom line is that we cannot go where we have not been given permission to go by God or leadership. In the Book of Acts, the seven sons of Sceva prayed for a demonized man using the name of Jesus. They were seriously beaten by the demonic spirit because they were not in submission or sent for that purpose by recognized leaders, presuming to have authority that they did not have (see Acts 19:14). They were simply not *known* in the realm of the Spirit. Anyone with even a slight understanding of God's process of promotion will not be eager to fake authority where they do not have it or presume authority where they have not been given it.

Another good test of our true authority is whether we would have the same level of Kingdom influence or authority if we no longer held our current position. Do we possess true Kingdom equity outside of our job or ministry title? Is our sphere of authority only tied to that to which we are connected? This may be God's exact purpose for us as we are clearly called to move together in tribes and connected families. However, these are important questions to answer as we correctly understand our Kingdom position.

Authority is delegated to us. Trying to gain authority through copying methods, style and tactics does not cause us to have authority in the realm of the Spirit. Soundforgers must be released to engage in new spheres of corporate prophetic and apostolic worship by God, leaders, and those ultimately responsible for the corporate gathering or setting. The bottom line is that wisdom requires us to walk exactly where we are within our given sphere of influence. Dutch Sheets puts it this way, "Beginning with your private world—conquer! Then in your extended world—overcome! And finally, in your universal world—rule!"[12]

Dutch Sheets also outlines seven principles that determine authority that help us to understand spheres of influence and authority in the realms of priestly, prophetic and apostolic worship:

1. *Our relationship to Christ* and our salvation. While each believer moves in different levels of authority for some activities, everyone has equal authority to access the Father in Jesus' name.

2. ***The principle of concentric expansion***. From our personal lives, to our churches, regions, and nations—as the circle expands outward, our personal authority decreases.

3. ***Our understanding of God and His Word***. Without knowledge of it we will not be aware of His provisions for us or of His ways through which they come. Obviously, if we are ignorant of what is rightfully ours through Christ, we will not exercise authority to lay hold of those provisions through faith.

4. ***Our connection to and identification with God's heart***. God gives authority to those who think the way He thinks and want what He wants.

5. ***Our ability to listen to God and discern His will***. Delegated authority has everything to do with representation. We receive authority from the one we represent.

6. ***The decisions of others.*** For example, sin in that person's life or an unresolved issue between him and God may affect how much authority I have to lay hold of a biblical promise for him.

7. ***Our assignment***. This is the authority that comes from representation. Though we all have the same level of

authority when it comes to accessing our Heavenly Father and petitioning Him for our personal needs in Christ's name, we do not walk in the same level of authority when it comes to fulfilling spiritual assignments.[13]

As we understand our position as the Apostolic Church—the *ekklesia*—our spheres of influence both individually and corporately are being defined and clarified. A local church filled with many individuals who have been trained in revelation of God's hatred toward sickness, know who they are in Christ, and have walked out overcoming in the area of healing and health will probably have corporate authority to move out into their neighborhoods and communities and heal the sick. Likewise, the boundaries in which worship leaders have operated are being expanded and our function clarified as a pure Kingdom paradigm is realized. Kingdom musicians must have understanding of their specific realm of influence and positioning, must be released by those that recognize their leadership, and must experience the necessary activation of the deposits of God within them.

Just as gatherings with different mandates will require different levels of authority and emphasis in leadership, this is also true for worship leaders and Soundforgers. A regional or city-wide gathering where city elders and apostles are functioning requires worship leaders who can operate within a city-wide jurisdiction. Some worship leaders will instinctively take the gathering into a deep place of devotion, and others will be used to sensitize the representatives to what God is saying and doing in the "now," partnering with five-fold ministries to help move the people into alignment. Neither one of these is nobler, but they have definite and distinct functions. However, only the appropriate application will accomplish the purpose for the gathering. Soundforgers must become available to move with God in releasing priestly, prophetic, or apostolic worship as the situation requires.

Although there are legitimate warnings to *individuals* operating outside of their God-ordained realm of authority, there is a dynamic found in *corporate gathering* that releases the church into greater authority and enables operation in a wider jurisdiction than normal. The release of corporate apostolic and prophetic anointings causes us to move as the Body beyond our usual sphere of assignment. The corporate gathering can—under the leading of God's Spirit—carry influence disproportionate to its size and the individuals who are present. Synergistically, the sum of the parts under the will of God is greater than the individual callings and anointings when operating alone.

Now we have laid a foundation about the Kingdom and the Government of God. We will take a look at Heaven's Word in the mouth of the apostolic church in the form of decrees and declarations.

ENDNOTES

1. Peter Wagner, *Spheres Of Authority* (Colorado Springs, CO: Wagner Publications, 2002), 27.

2. Kris Vallotton, *Apostleships*, Bethel School of the Prophets, August 10, 2006, Redding, CA.

3. Barbara J. Yoder, *The Breaker Anointing* (Ventura, CA: Regal Books, 2004), 15-17.

4. John Eckhardt, *Moving In the Apostolic* (Ventura, CA: Regal Books, 1999), 23.

5. Dr. Paula Price, *Eternity's Generals* (Tulsa, OK: Flaming Vision Publications, 2005), 6.

6. Dutch Sheets, *Authority in Prayer* (Bloomington, MN: Bethany House, 2006), 27-38.

7. Dutch Sheets, *Authority in Prayer* (Bloomington, MN: Bethany House, 2006), 61.

8. Peter Wagner, *Spheres Of Authority* (Colorado Springs, CO: Wagner Publications), 75-77.

9. Taken from a concept by Dr. Doug Stringer, Somebody Cares, Houston, TX.

10. Kris Vallotton, *Bethel School Of The Prophets*, Training Manual 2006, Redding, CA.

11. Kris Vallotton, *Prophets and Prophesy*, Bethel School of the Prophets, August 8, 2006, Redding, CA.

12. *Authority in Prayer*, 170.

13. *Authority in Prayer*, 150-166.

Chapter 6

Decrees & Declarations

"I will declare the decree of the Lord." —King David (See Psalm 2:7.)

Decree—an edict made by someone in authority, an order or judgment of a court.

Decreeing—to order, adjudge or ordain by decree.

From a Kingdom perspective, the Lord has always decreed from the beginning of creation to set in place the way things are in Heaven into the earth. Throughout history He has revealed Himself and His ways by raising various voices to carry His Word and His decree—Abraham, Moses, the Prophets, and ultimately His Son and His Church. It is clear from our understanding of governing legislation that governmental rulers and kings govern, bring order, protect, or enlarge the boundaries of their particular geography or institution by making decrees. In our current legislative structure decrees can be civil, ceremonial or judicial.

There are six primary biblical words for a decree,[1] and together they paint a rich picture of what we are referring to:

- a royal edict, commission, decree.

- to arrange, to speak, to subdue, declare, pronounce, a cause.

- a commandment, an enactment, appointment (of time, space), statute, necessary ordinance.

- a judgment, judicial sentence.

- something authoritatively spoken, an edict.

- a decree, to cut down, to cut off, to quarry or cut out.

The overarching theme speaks of a royal, necessary edict or commandment that is authoritative in content. It can be pronounced, declared, or spoken; and it commissions, sets in order, and subdues. Another interesting concept from these root words is to quarry or cut out—implying an ability to cut through, shape, and make a way. Kings make decrees throughout the Old Testament. The Psalms are full of them. Israel is threatened by Haman's decree. Ezra and Nehemiah are released to rebuild by one. Today, Jesus is making decrees over His Church and the nations of the earth.

In the Isaiah 22:22 passage, the Key of David shuts and opens. Keys in the Bible can be symbolic of a God-given decree. Just like a key, decrees are crafted instruments from one in authority that lock and unlock places of access and so by their very nature govern, control, and protect boundaries; they also release justice and limit or allow access. The key of David is set in the locks of our families, churches, regions, and nations waiting to be turned by the decree of the Lord and His triumphant Church. Dutch Sheets, again in *Authority in Prayer*, speaks of the position of God's Church, His *ekklesia* and their function to use the keys of the Kingdom:

> In this first decree about the Church, Jesus is saying that
> the Kingdom government (rule, decrees, council) of hell
> won't prevail over his Kingdom government on Earth—the
> Church. He follows this declaration by saying He would
> give to His ekklesia "keys" (see Matt. 16:19), which also
> bring to mind authority. Keys lock or unlock, in order to
> close or open, doors and gates. Christ's Church would have
> keys (authority) to lock the gates (government) of hell and
> release the gates (government) of Heaven.[2]

DECLARATIONS

For the purpose of clarity I want to make a distinction between
decrees and declarations. Because of the legislative nature of a
decree, we do not have authority to simply decree in every sphere we
choose. Our authority to make a decree is directly tied into our sphere
of authority and that which we have been given to rule and lead. The
greater the designated authority of an individual, the wider his or her
jurisdiction to make a decree. Simply, we can decree in any arena
where we have been given delegated authority and this obviously
begins with our own personal lives and families. An apostle set over
a region or entire denomination would have authority to make
decrees that pertained to that sphere. A group of apostles and
prophets gathered in a region with a specific assignment from God
would be able to make decrees over that geography in that setting

that an *individual* leader would not have the authority to do so. When the church is gathered together and given a discerned assignment, there are dimensions of corporate anointing that we are touching that enable us to move in higher dimensions of authority together than if we were operating alone. A declaration is a pronouncement of something already set in place by a previous decree. Generally, we would do better as believers in making a *declaration* based upon what the Word of God has already *decreed*, or proclaiming what apostles, prophets, and other five-fold leaders have already released and decreed.

Using the decrees and declarations given to us as the Church is one way we use the *Keys of the Kingdom*. In the original language, the passage in Matthew 16:19 that refers to this clearly implies: *Whatever you bind on Earth will **already have been** bound in Heaven, whatever you loose on Earth will **already have been** loosed in Heaven* (see Matt. 16:19). This speaks of us living and moving in revelation knowledge and enforcing the *now* of what the Lord has already decreed from Heaven. Allowing on the Earth only what is permissible in Heaven—insisting on joy instead of sorrow, peace in place of disorder, health for sickness, life in place of death. Psalm 149:4-7 reveals that this is available for all believers in the context of praise and worship:

> *For the Lord takes delight in His people; He crowns the humble with salvation. Let the saints rejoice in this honor and sing for joy on their beds. May the praise of God be in their mouths and a double-edged sword in their hands, to inflict vengeance on the nations* (Psalm 149:4-7).

The Lord's Prayer contains an incredible example of a declaration. It also carries a clear corporate emphasis—not focused on I, me, or my—but on we, our, and us. Jesus told us to pray this way! Matthew 6:10 says, "Thy kingdom come, thy will be done in earth as it is in heaven." When we unfold the Greek in this passage, it is actually an *imperative command*: "Come thy Kingdom, be done thy will." It is a corporate declaration of agreement calling for Earth to be aligned with the way things are in Heaven, acknowledging that His is the highest order. I am not saying that we simply "get what we say." Kingdom declarations begin and end within the heart and mind of God. He speaks first and we declare!

The deep things of God are being searched out by the Spirit and revealed. We speak these words taught by the Spirit because we have been given the mind of Christ (see 1 Cor. 2:10). I am not saying that our realities are never infused with difficulties. Neither am I stating that a decree or declaration is the only form of Kingdom communication. There are moments for breathtaking silence and contemplation, along with many other forms of connection with Heaven. However, it is imperative for us to push through passivity or an apathetic mindset that disables and diminishes our authority to understand our place in releasing the words and will of God into the earth.

A decree or declaration can also be released in the form of a blessing. Jesus clearly teaches us to pray for and bless our enemies (see Matt. 5:43-45). In the New Testament our battle is against spiritual forces and earthly systems rather than individuals (see Eph. 6:12). Moses' blessing over His sons in Deuteronomy 30 is a powerful weapon that I often speak over my natural and spiritual children. It releases a blessing of understanding who we are, releases the hand of God upon us, and in this alignment actively lifts us above certain aspects of warfare.

ORDER IN DECREES AND DECLARATIONS

Different levels of decrees and declarations are released to different levels of leadership in corporate gatherings. Remember, as believers we all have equal access to the Father through relationship with Jesus, but as individuals and churches and even corporate gatherings our giftings and assignments in God cover different spheres of influence. Our church's *7-11 Prayer Watch* often releases declarations over the geographic region that we believe marks our God-given territory—primarily the Dallas-Fort Worth Metroplex. In those times, as leaders we also make declarations over portions of our church body and individuals. These meetings are usually powerfully charged with the presence of God and priestly, prophetic, and apostolic worship partner together. However, a different level of authority would be realized in a gathering of nationally recognized leaders who felt called to merge their giftings and authority to make declarations of change over the nation or nations.

As we grasp our specific sphere of authority or the level of authority by association, we can then understand that there are different levels of decrees and declarations and a proper order in making them:

- *Decrees and Declarations by Individuals*–These are based on God's written or prophetic Word to you, your family and children, or over your physical body. They are based upon the atonement and finished work of Jesus, the written Word of God and biblical principles. We are required to consistently develop intimacy with God so that we can hear and make declarations based upon His Word, His voice, His call, and revealed will to us. Declarations can also be made by individuals in a gathering of the corporate Body based upon previous decrees given by five-fold leaders. As a father to two boys, I make declarations over them regularly based upon promises of God from His Word. They're decrees that are focused upon their protection, destiny, revelation, wisdom, and favor among other things. Taking my place of authority and making Spirit-led declarations over my children is a legitimate Kingdom function as a father.

- *Corporate Decrees and Declarations*–These are made by leaders or churches and enforce God's revealed will for a specific church body, city, or region and are often based upon Scripture or prophetic words.

- *Prophetic Decrees and Declarations*–Prophetic decrees pronounce and often foretell—revealing, at a specific junction in time, the mind of the Lord into the Earth, and activating the Body to respond. On May 28, 2005, Chuck Pierce gave a prophetic decree to England that he saw a sword in the heavens over London and England—that the nation was in a critical time and that the next 40 days would determine the reversal of the power of unbelief that was holding the Church captive in the nation.[3] On July 7, 2005, I was the assigned worship leader for a conference that began in London on the evening of several terrorist bombings in the city. These attacks happened on the 40th day after Chuck Pierce's word to the nation.[4] God revealed part of His purpose through a Prophet so that we could choose life as a nation at a difficult time.

Prophets enable the Church to become unified in one voice, moving in a Jeremiah 1:10 function: "…I appoint you over nations and Kingdoms to uproot and tear down, to destroy and overthrow, to build and to plant" (Jer. 1:10). We must listen to the prophets and discover what the Holy Spirit is saying prophetically to the Church and to our regions and begin to respond, intercede, and declare according to Heaven's word to us.

- *Apostolic Decrees and Declarations*–As we have discussed, true apostles have authority within their assigned sphere to make decrees for great advancement and breakthrough. One such example is Jay Swallow, the apostle and First Nations chief. In 2001, the Standing Rock Reservation in Dakota ranked number one for suicides amongst all of the Sioux tribe reservations. As a leader and apostle, Jay Swallow was led by the Holy Spirit to make a decree, dismantling the spirit of suicide from every corner of the Standing Rock Reservation. Since this time the suicide rate has diminished significantly amongst the Sioux Tribe in that reservation.

Corporate declaration songs released by prophetic and apostolic musicians may not be crafted as specifically as this one made by apostle Jay Swallow and may not reach out over a whole nation like the warning given by Chuck Pierce to England. However within our given sphere of influence, we are to grow in authority in releasing and restricting what happens in our families, churches, and communities on our watch. From the passages we have looked at, it is clear that as His representatives we are called to reign in His authority. At the appropriate times and under the direction of the Holy Spirit under godly leaders, it is necessary for us to see ourselves as a voice moving under His delegated authority corporately reinforcing decrees alongside apostles and prophets and proclaiming declarations that are centered on bringing Heaven's rule. We must understand that going to war or stating a decree of God's order is only necessary because we live in a fallen system where things are out of order with Creation's design. The very nature of the Kingdom is that it is here to displace all that is contrary to the will of God. We war and decree for the purpose of seeing Heaven's peace and order established.

Having looked at the function and role of apostles, the apostolic church, and decrees and declarations, we are now positioned to discuss

Apostolic Worship as a crucial dimension of worship that we are reclaiming in these days.

ENDNOTES

1.   *Strong's Concordance*, Hebrew 1881, 1696, 2706, 2942, 3982, 1510.

2.   Dutch Sheets, *Authority in Prayer*, 62.

3.   Chuck Pierce, God's Intervention over London and the Whole of England, Middlesex, England, May 28, 2005.

4.   On Thursday July 7, 2005, four suicide bombers later named as Hasib Hussain, Mohammad Sidique Khan, Germaine Lindsay and Shehzad Tanweer struck in central London, killing 52 people and injuring more than 770. (Source: http://news.bbc.co.uk, 14 May 2008.)

Apostolic Worship

Because of the mandates that God has set before us, the apostolic Church is rising to take its place in the realm of the Spirit. Just as in the songs of the Book of Psalms and in the Tabernacle of David, apostolic worship is again emerging as a vehicle for corporate declarations and decrees. As the corporate Church gathers in various ways aligned with the purposes of the Kingdom, the words of Heaven are being placed in our mouths that shift the way things are on the earth. Our level of influence as a corporate mouthpiece is increasing, and worship empowered with an apostolic dimension is being grafted in as part of this change. Just as with the priestly and prophetic dimensions of worship, the apostolic in worship is not a higher or more greatly desired place but simply has a different function. Whereas priestly worship is earth to Heaven, and prophetic worship focuses upon releasing revelation, apostolic worship moves from **Heaven to earth** in the form of a declaration or announcement. Apostolic worship carries authority and engages the Key of David like no other worship dimension.

MUSIC AND THE APOSTOLIC

Biblically, there are numerous examples both in the Old and New Testament of kings, leaders, prophets and apostles releasing various types of governing and impacting decrees and declarations, affecting both the natural and the spiritual dimensions. In terms of praise and worship, there are many places that certain Psalms carry an outward focus and "sent-ness" within their DNA. Some speak of decrees (see Ps. 2:7) and call for God to wake and decree (see Ps. 7:6b) and even refer to children being ordained to decree (see Ps. 8:2). There are also other examples where the psalmists themselves release decrees (see Ps. 2:10). Governing strategic declarations are powerful in releasing God's order and rule, and songs, or music itself, can be used as a vehicle for a decree. Psalm 2 is an incredible example of an apostolic Psalm.

Why do the nations conspire and the peoples plot in vain? The kings of the Earth take their stand and the rulers gather together against the Lord and against his Anointed One. "Let us break their chains," they say, "and throw off their fetters."

The One enthroned in Heaven laughs; the Lord scoffs at them. Then He rebukes them in his anger and terrifies them in his wrath, saying, "I have installed my king on Zion, my holy hill."

I will proclaim the decree of the Lord: He said to me, "You are my Son, today I have become your Father.

Ask of me, and I will make the nations your inheritance, the ends of the earth your possession. You will rule them with

an iron scepter; you will dash them to pieces like pottery."
Therefore, you kings, be wise; be warned, you rulers of the
earth. Serve the Lord with fear and rejoice with trembling. Kiss
the Son, lest he be angry and you be destroyed in your way, for
his wrath can flare up in a moment. Blessed are all who take
refuge in him (Psalm 2).

Psalm 2 moves almost entirely within an outward declaratory dimension. There is no place where it speaks directly to the Father. The author of this song is unknown, but historically understood to be a Psalm of David where he clearly exercises his position as King of Israel in releasing the government of God. From the beginning, it launches into an outward focus, questioning the position of earthly rulers and kingdoms. A declaration comes directly from God through the psalmist in verse 6, "I have installed my King on Zion, my holy hill," (Ps. 2:6) and verse 7 states, "I will proclaim the decree of the Lord" (Ps. 2:7)—clearly showing the psalmist as the one carrying the decree. Verses 8-10 illustrate the supremacy of Jesus in His relation to the kingdoms of earth (see Ps. 2:8-10). It ends speaking directly to the nations warning them to "Kiss the Son" (Ps. 2:12). What is crucial to understand is that this declaration was made originally by David to impact the realm of the Spirit—as not every earthly king could have physically heard this song in the natural. David makes declarations that set a mark down in the earth as to how things are from Heaven's perspective. This apostolic song became part of Israel's hymn collection for generations as a spiritual declaration. Other factors that contribute to the apostolic nature of this Psalm are the levels of influence that it engages. In the first three verses nations, peoples, kings and rulers set themselves against God (see Ps. 2:1-3). They conspire, plot, stand, and gather together. These are not passive thoughts but definitive actions. The psalmist releases declarations that answer these plans clearly, authoritatively, and with dominion. Today, influential realms of spiritual and earthly power are actively engaged in plans to overthrow the rule of the Lord. The Father's response is that He will give the nations to us as an inheritance and a possession. As modern-day psalmists, Soundforgers have a purpose-filled role to play in partnering with the decrees of Jesus across the earth.

Psalm 68 also carries insight into corporate apostolic proclamation:

> *The Lord announced the word, and great was the company of those that proclaimed it: Kings and armies flee in haste; in the camps men divide the plunder* (Psalm 68:10-12).

It is not specified, but in being consistent with Old Testament leadership function, a prophet would have announced the Word of the Lord which was then proclaimed by the king and his armies. The result of this apostolic declaration is the overthrow and disbanding of kings and armies and the plundering of His enemy's resources.

Psalm 24 also needs mentioning as it highlights a key function of apostolic worship in this season:

> *Lift up your heads, O you gates; be lifted up, you ancient doors, that the King of glory may come in* (Psalm 24:7).

Corporate apostolic worship is to declare to cities and regions to *open up* for God's presence to come in. Soundforgers are not just ministering to the Father's heart and welcoming Him or providing an atmosphere where the Church can soak in Heaven, but are declaring Heaven's word to ancient doors that they must open and receive the glory of God. It is incredible how we are called to work with Him, both as friends and joint heirs.

APOSTOLIC WORSHIP

Apostolic worship evolves from prophetic revelation and is a vehicle for the activation of declarations from Heaven into the earth. Key characteristics are:

1. It *calls this realm into order and causes shifts* from Heaven's perspective, stating, "Your will be done on earth as it is in heaven" (Matt. 6:10).

2. It operates at the spiritual *hinge-places* of our corporate gatherings.

3. Because of its nature, it *legislates* in the earth.

4. Apostolic worship breaks through all that is not of God to *reinstate the Kingdom's presence and rule as a reality.*

5. Its content is often focused upon issues of regional or

national geographic consequence related to the *establishment of God's Kingdom and purpose.*

Apostolic worship (within various assignments and under different spheres of influence) can speak to nations and kingdoms, their rulers and armies, focuses on issues of authority, foreign gods, states and establishes Heaven's dominion, and declares justice and the displacement of injustice. Different types of apostolic music that are emerging include:

- Sounds that carry the government of God, expressing the sound of Heaven for the moment, representing what the Holy Spirit is saying and doing in a given setting.

- Music and declaration songs that converge with spoken decrees by apostles and prophets.

- Spontaneous or already written songs that are governing or foundational in subject matter and focus that are sung for a season by the corporate. They focus upon the non-negotiable truths of the Kingdom and cause apostolic expansion and release to the church.

UNDERSTANDING APOSTOLIC WORSHIP

Apostolic worship is still Father-centered but *alignment* focused—taking the scepter and government of God and declaring its supremacy. It exists to see the increase of His government and peace, which was prophesied by Isaiah, forever expanding (see Isa. 9:7-8). It is corporate, it is governmental, it takes territory, it legislates, and it carries authority within its DNA.

Using the Key of David symbolism, apostolic worship harvests from the storehouse of prophetic revelation and crafts a *key* that unlocks and locks places of strategic importance in the earth. Among other things already mentioned, apostolic worship is used to enforce Heaven's rule, to bring change, to seal a transition place, to release justice, to open regions to the presence of God, and to displace foreign gods. Just as individual apostles out of a place of humility, character, and the Father's heart are given authority to govern and break through, so the Bride in *corporate worship* is called to move from her place of priestly intimacy to becoming a unified voice. Where priestly worship *engages* the church as a captivated Bride, apostolic worship *activates* her as a Kingdom carrier.

Kingdom decrees are being made from Heaven by Jesus Christ, and we are sounding them as His *ekklesia* in prophetic and apostolic worship and declarations. This is requiring us to operate in greater understanding of the authority He has invested in us as the Church. Because of his authority, an earthly ruler will sometimes be required to go to war. Other circumstances will demand legislation in the form of decrees and declarations. Both are valid functions of his position as a ruler. Jesus moved in perfect synchronization with Heaven and walked in authority because He spoke and acted based upon the revealed will of His Father. Declarations from the mouth of Jesus through His Bride have authority, not because they sound powerful or carry the vocabulary of authority, but because they are based upon the revealed strategy of the Father at their very core. The Lord knows the transition moment to turn each and every situation for His purpose in our cities and nations. With every moment that passes, bowls of intercession (see Rev. 5:8) become filled with the prayers of the generations and the Father announces that the time for change has arrived. Apostolic worship resonates with announcements from Heaven and is different from the priestly because it is not functioning to *fill* the bowls in Heaven but to *declare the answer* and see powerful groundbreaking results.

Decrees given by apostles often speak into arenas that are outside of local church jurisdiction. Likewise, corporate apostolic worship carries content that is outward and by its very nature invades territory. Like any other God-given declaration, apostolic songs literally set things in order in the Spirit realm. We must understand that worship *from the earth* will be continually offered and that spontaneous songs that minister to *individuals* in a particular gathering and touch people in that setting are valid. However, we are in a time where it is crucial for the release of governing songs coming *from Heaven*, that have a wider jurisdiction and that touch subjects and places outside of those present in the room—just as we see in the Psalm 2 example.

I want to clarify a point here regarding a warfare paradigm. As we know, some significant engagements with the enemy were won in partnering directly with worship in the Old Testament (see Isa. 30:31-33, 2 Chron. 20:20-27). However, we are not simply presuming a warfare stance in these days, but something different—a prophetic and apostolic Kingdom paradigm. This *includes* warfare as Heaven directs—but cannot simply be contained in a warfare paradigm alone.

Governing apostolic worship is concerned with releasing the fullness of God's presence and revealed strategy in God's now moment through corporate declaration—establishing, building, and enforcing the complete authority of Heaven based upon a New Covenant, post-Resurrection reality. More than spiritual warfare, we are called to hear and declare what He is declaring over various arenas. Rather than coming *against* spiritual forces we are releasing Heaven's word that brings the answer and the presence of God. Sometimes the King is releasing perfect mercy and at other times perfect justice.

We need to see gifts in the apostolic Church unlocked and anointings married to see His Kingdom come on Earth as it is in Heaven. The new breed of Psalmist that walks as a Heaven-hearer will secure great progress for the Kingdom of God in the days ahead as they release apostolic worship. Whether the role of the Soundforger is supporting and surrounding a prophet and apostle with governing sounds and music or releasing a song so that the corporate can declare, they must take their place.

> *Just as the priestly dimension in worship is the ultimate place of personal expression and the prophetic dimension is the hinge-place of revelation, so apostolic worship is the ultimate place of corporate expression.*

MODELED IN HEAVEN

In Chapter 5 of the Book of Revelation we find examples of priestly, prophetic and apostolic songs in the context of worship.

In verses 8-10, the 24 elders sing a **new song** with harps and bowls (see Rev. 5:8-10). This song speaks of Jesus' governmental position—His purchase of those on the Earth and their call to reign and carry His government. They release a declaration song gathered up from the petitions of the earth over the kingdoms. This is the nature of *apostolic worship.*

In verse 11, we see *prophetic worship* as Heaven, through the song of many angels calls earth to come into alignment with the reality of who the Lamb is—that He will receive power and wealth and wisdom and strength (see Rev. 5:11-12). They are calling earth into understanding and affirming that this is truth, that He is worthy to receive all that the earth esteems.

In verse 13, we see *priestly Earth to Heaven worship*—where every creature in Heaven and on Earth and under the Earth and on the sea sings a priestly song of devotion to the Father and Son (see Rev. 5:13).

THREE STRANDS TODAY

Today, as New Testament musicians, as we sing psalms, hymns, and spiritual songs to one another (see Eph. 5:19) there is a release and inclusion of different types and dimensions of corporate songs into corporate worship. In past decades, we have honored singing psalms and hymns, but we are now discovering new levels of what it means to experience spiritual songs. The equipment that emerging Soundforgers carry is causing a fresh increase of new songs—be they priestly, prophetic, or apostolic. They are either spontaneous or pre-written, but carry the DNA of something the Holy Spirit is releasing in the moment that enables them to connect the purposes of Heaven with the earth in a profound way.

Many groups of worshipers have encouraged environments for priestly worship to emerge. The Vineyard Churches along with countless others have honored God through extended times of intimate worship in the corporate and have ushered in an incredible priestly Bridal paradigm that has been instrumental in seeing much of the Body of Christ regain intimacy in worship. They have consistently modeled a closeness with the Father that seeks encounter in worship at whatever cost. We go beyond merely singing affectionate words into actually interacting and experiencing His touch, presence, and nearness. An adjustment needs to be made in the way we approach a lifestyle of worship—where the encounter is the starting place for the corporate gathering, not the arrival place. Likewise, along with this increase in intimacy, the sound coming out of many lead worshipers and teams has been militant and invading. Certain churches, ministries, and movements have been instrumental in forerunning in the place of authentic prophetic and declaratory worship in the last decade—clearly modeling revelatory and governing worship.

It is not my goal to reach a closed definition of the three strands of priestly, prophetic, and apostolic worship but simply to begin to discuss and enlarge the place of our understanding of what the Holy Spirit is releasing. As I was speaking with the Lord about worship leading, He said to me very clearly, "There is an anointing to enlarge the devotional life of an individual, and there is an anointing to change the government of a situation." The corporate Bride of Christ is more powerful than she realizes as she stands before the Lord, hears His heart, and in turn proclaims it into the earth.

As I have led worship cross-denominationally, cross-generationally, and cross-culturally, I have personally experienced the release of priestly, prophetic, and apostolic worship in various degrees in different settings. I have learned through mistakes to be sensitive to leadership and to determine ahead of time the degree to which the specific group I am leading is ready, or is carrying authority, to move into revelatory or declarative worship. Lending ourselves to a pastoral mindset at times and moving a group from A to B may be more effective than trying to begin at D and drag them through Z.

I have led worship several times for an annual national conference bringing together branches of a particular ministry from all over the United Kingdom and Europe. During my first introduction to the leadership, they clearly communicated that it was a time of transition for the ministry. I had sensed ahead of time that this was the case and had prepared myself for possible prophetic and declaratory songs as specific revelation, Scriptures and phrases were laid upon my heart. I gathered these together along with my song list. Because the leadership of this ministry were committed to moving the corporate forward in spontaneous prophetic and governing worship, I was open to see how these phrases and thoughts that I felt the Lord was speaking could be woven into songs within our worship or spoken out. Our corporate worship times were charged with momentum and life because of the prophetic and apostolic dimension that was released as we worshiped. I was given authority by leadership to consider our sessions a safe and appropriate environment to stretch corporate boundaries out as they were clearly set aside for *corporate progress* and not just *personal devotion*. Overall, during several sessions, there was a combination of the three strands we have talked about. Some were clearly charged with a pastoral, priestly anointing , and so worship was allowed to remain in this dimension. Other times required that declarations be formed and released as Heaven's specific mandates became clear. Remember prophetic and apostolic worship do not negate intimacy or devotion but harvest what is revealed by the Spirit of God and move the corporate into *greater recognition* of what is on the Lord's heart by putting it into song and therefore into *greater activation.*

Prayer for the Nations, pioneered by our friends and mentors Rod and Julie Anderson, is a UK-based strategic intercessory ministry that prays for London, for the nation, and its government. Over several years in partnering with God for our nation, we often experienced dynamic dimensions of priestly, prophetic, and apostolic worship being released and woven together on a regular basis in the house of prayer that was pioneered less than half a mile away from Parliament. Many declarations were released in songs from the corporate nameless group that met there legislating the truth of the Kingdom of God into the city. I remember on one occasion singing over our Prime Minister a song from the heart of God, urging him to be wise in the Father's eyes at the expense of all else. The group picked up on this focus and began to sing and declare, pray, and proclaim the reality of this man coming into a new place of godly wisdom and counsel. We also often upheld him and surrounded him with prayers of protection too, but on this particular day there was an urgency to speak over him a new dimension of wisdom in governing. We will probably never know exactly what was happening, but there was a strong sense that something had been accomplished. We had moved from approaching the Father in a priestly dimension, through hearing and understanding prophetically what was on His heart, to finally declaring His purpose—all in the context of a flow of praise and worship.

Apostolic worship is often released at crucial times and seasons. As I mentioned in the previous chapter, I was assigned as the lead worshiper for a conference in the heart of London that started on the evening of horrific terrorist bombings in London. Several internationally recognized apostolic and prophetic leaders including Dutch Sheets, Chuck Pierce, Tom and Jane Hamon, Rod and Julie Anderson, and Sharon Stone joined with the British Church from all over the nation to make declarations of hope and national identity. A corporate group of lovers of God drove the perspective of Heaven into the spiritual atmosphere over a traumatized and violated city. The truth of Heaven and the rule of His Kingdom in that Christian nation were lifted over and above the act of terrorism and fear. Where false religion and terrorism were making a declaration over London, the Lion of Judah roared through His Church and had the final word. The declarations made were neither appeasing, apathetic, nor submissive; but were apostolic, prophetic, and powerful in pushing back a violent and unlawful attack. We do pray for our enemies, forgive and bless individuals and seek to reach all cultures with Christ-like love, but do not tolerate the spirits at work through demonic spiritual structures and terrorist agendas.

While undergirding a time of intercession at *The Call: England*, a gathering of almost 20,000 in Reading, England, leadership sensed a call to see the Body rise to a new place of standing in its authority to contend for the land. This was a prayer gathering specifically focused upon a day of prayer and fasting for the future of our nation. We had prayed much and prepared our hearts for a day of consecration and change. Our team released a song inspired by a power-filled prophetic declaration from Julie Anderson that simply said, "We will go to war." This was extremely powerful as several thousand people began to declare this in unison. This obviously served to cement what the Holy Spirit was releasing in the "now" of the gathering. However because the Lord is not surprised by international events, I personally believe that this agreement and declaration were preparing the ground in the spirit for the "War on Terrorism" as Britain would later waiver in her decision to participate. I am not saying that I endorse everything that happened during that season in the Middle East, but we are in a time in the nations that the Lord will have no foreign gods ruling over people groups and nations that He has created and destined with purpose.

Another example of corporate declaration came at *The Call: Texas* where a cry of "shift, shift, shift, shift" began to rise up from a small group of people unprompted by those on the platform. This grew and grew as hundreds more individuals joined and continued for several minutes. The Spirit of God is initiating waves of declaration over the future of our cities and nations. Whether we remain passive or engage in partnering with Heaven will influence the transformation of cities, regions, and nations in the days ahead.

What he opens no one can shut, and what he shuts no one can open (Revelation 3:7).

Chapter 8

Navigating the Current Season

The purpose of *Emerging Worship* so far has been to explore priestly, prophetic, and apostolic worship while speaking identity and purpose to a new breed of Soundforgers who bring the influence of Heaven into the earth. As these three strands of worship emerge and merge into our corporate gatherings, we will have choices to make regarding the inclusion of revelatory and governing music and declarations. The priestly dimension with an earth-to-Heaven focus is making way for prophetic revelation from Heaven's perspective. Apostolic worship and declaration are evolving from this revelation and result in a Heaven-to-earth offensive. As we journey and transition it is crucial that we are able to navigate with clarity, locating where we are and where He is taking us.

TRANSITION

Although a place of limitless possibility, a place of transition carries with it the greatest potential to abort the future and retain the status quo. What we will ultimately forfeit if we do not recognize and engage the new season will only be revealed by history. In our cities, day after day, thousands worship at the altars of abortion, murder, and perversion. Idols of fame and success are given extravagant offerings as we bow to the giftedness of man and worship outward perfection. War rages in the nations, terrorist threats continue against several of our major cities, yet prayer as a source of national dependence has been removed from our public school system. We invite representation from every false religion to open Senate with a prayer to gods we do not know, but will not cry out and acknowledge the Justice bearer who will respond in mercy to what we will ask of Him. Many individuals, groups, and institutions are making ungodly declarations over the future of the nations—but we are called to rise, declare and enforce the revealed will of God.

What will be the prepared response of the apostolic Church and God's Soundforgers in the coming seasons?

The invasion of Heaven's Kingdom and the presence of the King is needed in our cities and regions more than ever. The Church is called to engage Heaven *and* our communities, and there are signs that we are awakening. God's generals are hearing the voice of the warrior Bridegroom and speaking His decrees into the earth. These strategic announcements are marked with ability to break through into spiritual and geographic arenas that have been previously locked or closed to the people of God. The Church, saturated with the power and presence of God, is moving with the Kingdom mandates of Heaven and walking out the answers to ungodly plans for our cities. The sick are being healed and treasured destinies relocated. The Key of David has been placed on the shoulders of the Body with

Christ as the head. Declarations are being formed in the mouths of Soundforgers and are being released in apostolic worship as in many of the Psalms. In reviewing what we have already discovered, this is purpose-driven worship that is not passive, resting, soaking and self serving, but is invasive, urgent, counteractive, legislative and effective. Sounds and songs are emerging that literally rip away apathy and disengagement. In corporate worship, we have often wrongly defaulted to intimacy and rest as the only preparation place for the Body of Christ. This will never be taken from us—but comfort, retreat, sentiment, and the experience of intimacy alone will not equip the Church for what is already here or for what is coming in our cities and nations.

We have been beholding Him as Savior, Lover, and Friend, but He is revealing Himself increasingly in these days as the Lion, the Man of War, the Master of Breakthroughs, and the God of Justice. The "Who is this?" in Song of Solomon 6:10 reveals the beauty of One who captivates and romances us (see Song of Sol. 6:10). Equally, the "Who is this?" in Isaiah 63:1 reveals the One who is robed in garments stained in crimson, fierce and exceptional in the greatness of His strength— speaking in righteousness and mighty to save (see Isa. 63:1). He is both beautiful and terrible, an intimate lover and a strategist at war. He quiets us with His love and sings over us (see Zeph. 3:17) while releasing sounds of war to confirm that it is time to subdue our enemies (see 2 Sam. 5:22-25). God's corporate army is rising in the earth and is breaking through as He breaks through before us (see Mic. 2:13).

Our attitude determines whether we will be early, mid, or late adopters within the unfolding plan of God and whether we will, in actuality, move from vision to the possession of what He is releasing to us. We must embrace the current expression of God, catching the wave of what He is releasing regardless of whether we completely perceive it with our natural minds. We can never ultimately define what is *now* by an old paradigm because it is new! Many of us are like Jacob, asleep at Bethel, and completely unaware of the commencement of a new season. We have, however, found ourselves dreaming of spiritual gates and doors that access Heaven. Just like Jacob, we are not aware that the place where we sleep is the house of God and the gate of Heaven where angelic activity is moving to fulfill the plan of the Father.

> [Jacob] *came to a certain place and spent the night there, because the sun had set; and he took one of the stones of the place and put it under his head, and lay down in that place. He had a dream, and behold, a ladder was set on the earth with its top reaching to heaven; and behold, the angels of God were ascending and descending on it. Then Jacob woke from his sleep and said, "Surely the Lord is in this place, and I did not know it." He was afraid and said, "How awesome is this place! This is none other than the house of God, and this is the gate of heaven"* (Genesis 28:11-12,16-17 NASB).

We must now recognize our "certain place" as the "visitation place" where angels are ascending and descending—releasing Heaven's atmosphere and assignments. Jacob shifted into alignment with his purpose when he understood that the geography which the ladder was placed on was connected with a mandate from God for him and his descendants. We are becoming revitalized to know that Heaven is open, not only over us as individuals but over cities and geographic regions. We are consistently being sensitized to the *place* we are in as a global Body—the place of being called to live from Heaven to earth, the place of the Church as the gate of Heaven, the place of taking hold of the mandate of God and possessing the gates of our enemies (see Gen. 24:60), our cities, and our nations.

In corporate worship, as those who seek to live in constant awareness of the presence and voice of God, we stand as a point of faith in the earth realm where access to Him is secured and an open Heaven is reality. Worshipers are shifting in function from remaining only as a priesthood that minister **to** Him to engaging in strategic prophetic and apostolic governing worship that God is releasing **from** Him as part of the tabernacle worship that is being restored. Priestly, prophetic and apostolic worship are blending; the songs of earth and Heaven are joining together to release a sound that is awakening Creation.

A vision regarding the move from intimacy to strategy is significant in helping us to understand the transition we are in corporately:

> *…I noticed that there was another door in the weeping room. I asked the Lord what was behind that door and He told me that was where the Strategy Room was. As He said those words, instantly in my spirit I knew in that room divine strategy for end-time revival was available. Although*

the door was still closed, I recognized that Wisdom and Rev-elation were in there. Heavenly blueprints were laid out to see the fulfillment of His Kingdom coming to Earth from that room. It was like the hidden room that everybody searches for. Everyone longs to have divine strategy. I immediately asked if I could go in there and the Lord soberly told me that I didn't fit through the door. I instantly understood that I had to spend time in the weeping room. As I began to really apprehend the heart of God for the poor and the broken, issues of my soulish nature would be stripped away until I would become small enough to fit through the door.

At that moment everything became clear. This was the only way to access divine strategy. From the place of inti-macy, God invites us in to a deeper level—He beckons us into the weeping room—a place where we choose to see what He sees and feel what He feels. And as we spend time getting the heart of God, things of our flesh begin to be stripped away until we are small enough to fit through the door that leads to the strategy room.

...I believe that God is now moving many in the Church from the place of intimacy into weeping. This will lead them into the strategy room. In actuality, you never have to leave the intimacy room; you just discover the deeper levels. Many have already surrendered themselves to the weeping room and extravagantly pursued the heart of God for the broken—they are now being invited into the strategy room.

I had another encounter a little over a year ago in which I heard a loud voice say, "It's time!" and in the Spirit I saw the strategy room door swing open. God is inviting us into divine strategy that will release a global harvest of souls, and establish the revelation of His Kingdom on Earth through overcoming saints.[1]

A prophetic and apostolic people are being given access to the secrets of the Bridegroom's heart—not only in terms of compassion and mercy but also in terms of incredible strategy, the power of His presence and intense declaration that unlock earthly structures and even nations.

Soundforgers have been invited into the weeping room of intimacy and are now gaining strategic insight and understanding that is marking their music with the "now" of God. As listeners for, and capturers of the heartbeat of God—with a palette of sound available that can access either priestly, prophetic, or apostolic worship—they are equipped to give expression to the voice of this Bridegroom Warrior.

The Church is moving from the Bridal into the governmental. In actuality, I believe that He is marrying them together and releasing the union as a new wineskin. It is not a choice between *either* Bridal intimacy *or* governmental authority—but the converging of both.

ENGAGING IN STRATEGIC PURPOSE

Understanding given to me in a dream highlights further the importance of strategic worship in this season:

As I walked through the inside of a government underground bunker, a man whom I recognized as Winston Churchill walked with me. He expressed the intent to buy me a wrist-watch, and as we approached a table covered with contemporary watches from the best manufacturers in the world, I scanned the timepieces. Churchill did not look impressed and instead moved over to a side table that was covered with 1940s wartime pocket watches. He suddenly looked excited and said firmly, "This is much better."

The Lord is offering this generation an "understanding of the times" of the kind that Churchill carried in World War II. This is being revealed in supernatural measures of strategy, truth, and legislative declaration. There is an urgency in our nations that is not unlike pre-World War II Europe, as terrorism and ungodly agendas seek to infiltrate our thinking and establish fear. The name "Church-hill" also resonates that the Church is a light on a hill that cannot and will not be hidden (see Matt. 5:14) and the mountain of the Lord is being lifted above all other mountains (see Isa. 2:2). We are clearly in a season of a "war-watch" in the Church and the nations. This is timely revelation that can help us awaken, relocate, and function differently in the days ahead.

A crucial element of David's anointing was his ability to see God as a war strategist. As he inquired of the Lord, David became an intentional man of war who received specific strategies in dealing with anything that came to diminish or contend with the Kingdom of God in the earth. Strategy is so important because it carries the details of successful battle implementation in a war situation. Hebrews 11:32 speaks of the ancient heroes of the faith as those that conquered kingdoms, administered justice, and gained what was promised. Today, there are conquering strategies being released to those who will dare to partner with God in love and justice, as He deconstructs the kingdoms of this world.

Just as it required all 12 tribes to engage in dispossessing their enemy, so the Lord is positioning strategic gift mixes in relationship and geographic location for breakthrough in particular arenas. His apostolic people are positioned and ready. Although at times God's moving will appear to be unexpected and sudden, His purposes are rooted in His eternal plans to bring justice and righteousness into the nations.

> *In faithfulness He will bring forth justice; He will not falter*
> *or be discouraged till he establishes justice on the earth*
> (Isaiah 42:3b-4).

Throughout the earth, the Body is becoming increasingly aware that we have been drawn into a deeper level of Father-initiated maturing in order to make way for the release of a strategic Kingdom-demonstration generation. We are living in a moment where immaturity, divisions, bondages, and an over-focus upon one particular slant are being exposed and pried out of the hand of the Church. In every facet of ministry expression—including praise and worship—the maturing continues, transition takes place and the "big picture" takes its rightful position. Whether the over-focus slants toward ambition, doctrine, platforms of humanity, the contemporary, or the traditional, it is time for the presence and power of God, pure Kingdom ministry, alignment with the five-fold, and the activation of apostolic anointing and purpose. This Kingdom perspective being released to the Body of believers worldwide is putting all things into context—including our traditions, denominational emphasis, and some of the anointings we have begun to touch and experience.

In terms of strategic purpose, the mandates given to the Church that we discussed in Chapter 5 still remain as a blueprint for us. As God's children and apostolic people, we are created and called to subdue and rule over creation with Christ. Adam heard His voice in unbroken intimacy but engaged in a purpose filled specific task and function within creation design. What are God's Soundforgers called to subdue in this season and generation? To what mountains are you to cry, "Grace! Grace!" (see Zech. 4:7 NASB). To which of the places long devastated are you to cry, "Restore! Restore!" Overtaken by the zeal of the Lord, the courage of Phineas is again emerging in our generation to stop the plagues that are overtaking our cities and regions (see Num. 16:46-49, 25:1-10). The spirit of prophecy and apostolic declaration is here to subdue the spirit of the world, not merely for the purpose of confrontation but for restitution, justice, restoration, and reformation.

THE ATMOSPHERE OF HEAVEN

The new breed of emerging Psalmists are called to release the atmosphere of Heaven. Wherever the Body of Christ gathers is to be a place where Heaven and earth interact. Touchdown is happening in streets, buildings, businesses, malls, parks, hospitals, or even churches if necessary! The nature of Heaven is to invade earth. It happened over 2,000 years ago as Jesus released the Kingdom everywhere He went. It is happening today all over the earth.

We have to remain clear that engaging the three strands of priestly, prophetic and apostolic worship are secondary to the higher purpose of seeing Heaven released upon the Earth. In fact, His manifest glory *is* the point. We are giving ourselves to seeking and following a Person and His presence—not a formula. The time in which we live demands that we not engage another ministry method but live to see the atmosphere change in regions as we partner with Heaven in every sphere of society. As Soundforgers, our part is to worship our Father, host Him, hear His voice and decree His will to see the presence of the Glorious One established over geographic areas. The sounds and songs of Heaven, because of their very nature, *carry* the atmosphere of Heaven within their DNA. We are not after releasing the song of the Lord so much as we are after the atmosphere that releases the prophetic and apostolic over an entire room, city or region. In First Samuel 19:20, three groups of unregenerated people are overcome by the presence of God as the prophets and musicians work together. We can see the backslidden and unregenerated pre-Christian come into an encounter with God by standing and releasing the atmosphere of Heaven.[2] Kingdom businesses, street-prophets, media-visionaries, evangelists, and miracle workers will accelerate the Kingdom in their sphere of influence, saying what *they* hear to say, and doing what *they* see to do. Emerging worshipers simply have to do their part.

Apostolic worship has a *sent-ness* about it—a commitment to His purpose that attracts the Presence of God. We are invited to bring the attributes of God into the earth—taking a prevailing atmosphere and bringing Heaven's. There is no sickness, disease, depression, murder, or death in Heaven. It is therefore unlawful in the earth. I believe that the Father is poised and waiting to open up floodgates over our neighborhoods and nations if we will stand before Heaven and worship to see the atmosphere of Heaven released.

PARTNERING FOR SOCIETAL TRANSFORMATION

We are discovering what it looks like for the Body of Christ to be prepared to impact every sphere of society for transformation. We have been primarily discussing the sounds and songs of Heaven within the Church realm. Fresh creativity and perspective is being released as to how Soundforgers and the declarations and songs of Heaven can be infused into all arenas of culture and society.

We must allow ourselves to be expanded to dream of the multiple ways that Kingdom music can be released. In the arenas of media and arts and entertainment alone, the possibilities are endless: music carrying the DNA of Heaven filling film and television; fashion shows accompanied by sound and lyrics that recapture the captured; music producers forging the new and unheard industry songs that awaken a generation and speak to the deeper human condition; coffee-house psalmists that function locally and organically, fusing community with God-songs. Andy Hunter, a sound designer and DJ from the UK[3] is an incredible example of a voice in the marketplace. You have heard his sound partnered with some of Hollywood's mega movies. His music and lyrics are saturated with prophetic symbols and relevant parables to a generation. It is a distinctive sound—organic, relevant, and very Kingdom.

We know of several Kingdom businesses that engage a multifaceted approach in the marketplace. One such company employs intercessors and pastors alongside several hundred employees. They fuse prophetic intercession and insight with business principles. Nights of worship and ministry where strategy is infused into their sphere is a natural part of their operation. They are taking advantage of the synergy that Heaven is releasing for societal transformation.

The early Church also experienced the power of the synergy of Heaven and earth as it moved under the delegated authority of the Kingdom of God and the atmosphere of Heaven. Mark 16:19-20 highlights the power of the early Church as the Lord *worked with them*. The root of the word "worked" is the word we use today for "synergy." [4] In the activity of the early Church, Jesus had already ascended, and when the Holy Spirit descended the synergy was released that propelled the early church into exponential growth and influence. This is available to us today! [5]

There is a release of synergy as we partner with Heaven and merge our *spheres* as well as our *individual* callings, anointings, and giftings. No one individual, church, business, or ministry is equipped to maneuver us into societal transformation, but we will find our ultimate purpose in partnership, not only with Heaven, but also with each other. God gave me a vision that highlighted the aspect of humility and partnership for the advancement that is coming in our cities in the nations:

The large and ancient gate that stood before me was ornate and ominous. I presumed that it was the gate of the city. Surrounding me, many people were attempting to access entry by seemingly legitimate commands and spiritual tactics, but the gate would not open. Suddenly I heard a voice that spoke to me and said, "There is only one way to gain entry. It is reserved for those who have a certificate of humiliation." As these legal papers were handed over, the gate opened and I found myself inside what was actually a storage room that literally held thousands of keys. Some of them were large and ornate and others were small, dull and insignificant. All had labels. "Youth Movement," "Healing," and "Revival" were some that impacted me as I curiously scanned the room. Those who had gained entry were extremely excited as they realized the potential that this room held. They pushed through to grasp the keys which resonated with their hearts' cry. In the farthest corner of the room I saw a tiny key with a label that said "No Reputation." When I reached and picked it up, the key grew very large and heavy, and the label changed to the word "Government." Only then I recognized this as the key to the gate of the city. As the scene changed, I found myself standing before the gate of the city where I attempted to use this key of governmental authority—but I could not turn it in the huge lock alone. I heard the voice speak to me again—"it takes a government to open a governmental door." I then felt the presence of representatives of the five-

fold ministry gathered around the key, and together we
opened the gate of the city.

Soundforgers who have walked through seasons of being
humiliated in the arenas of man are being offered the keys of no reputation. In revealing His pleasure in "no reputation" the Lord is not
seeking a self-debasing religious posture, but a *trading-up* into all
that we were created for––a shift where our personal agenda and
"reputation" in the eyes of man are exchanged for massive moves of
the Kingdom of God. In place of our individualistic achievement,
something that only team synergy in partnership with Heaven can
release. If we, along with the Body of Christ will pick up these keys, we
will find ourselves holding the governmental Key of David, ready to
partner together in something that is bigger than us for the transformation of our communities and cities.

My home city of Dallas-Forth Worth completed 40 days of city-
wide prayer and fasting for the re-digging of the wells of revival in
our geographic region and in our generation. Although called into
mobilization and wonderfully guided under the leadership of Cindy
Jacobs and Generals International, this call from Heaven was not
about an individual, a ministry, or a particular denomination. Over 60
churches participated and actively locked into 24/7 fasting, worship,
strategic intercession, and declaration targeting the Metroplex. Many
healings took place during the ten nights of miracle meetings that
concluded the fast. Many fresh dimensions of priestly, prophetic, and
apostolic worship were released throughout the 40 days. The emphasis by the end of the fast was the unleashing of an empowered army

onto the streets to see the power of God and hope released into the most hopeless situations.

In wanting to affect our communities, God is currently activating a fresh wave of *prophetic evangelism* where the Body of Christ is being saturated by Heaven, receiving revelation, and going onto the streets and into communities to treasure hunt for the lost and reclaim the Father's inheritance. Soundforgers are partnering with this wave of evangelism because they have tools that welcome an atmosphere in worship where the prophetic can be activated and received. Apostolic worship over regions is causing shifts in the very atmosphere as we discussed in the incident at Pentecost. Soundforgers release the sound— hearts awaken— and the Body of Christ moves as God carriers to reap the harvest. Mercy and compassion ministries are also moving into the streets in our nations—touching the impoverished, poor, and homeless. My friend Ed Delph, founder of NationStrategy, speaks of an expectancy to see the lost in our communities worship God more profoundly than the Church. He bases this out of the Scripture in Matthew 5:16—they will see your good deeds and glorify your Father in Heaven.[6] It is time for the lost to see God as we engage in releasing Him in practical ways. Have you asked yourself what apostolic worship should sound like on the streets of our cities? Just as David "recovered all" in First Samuel 30 when he realized the enemy had touched the community and taken captive wives and children, so today there is a violent recovering mandate—an apostolic mantle—upon this generation to see cities and regions restored. The Key of David is in the locks of the gates and doorways to our cities and His government is emerging through his consecrated apostolic Church and listening Soundforgers.

USING THE KEY OF DAVID

These are the words of Him who is Holy and true, who holds
the key of David. What he opens no one can shut, and what
he shuts no one can open (Revelation 3:7b).

In navigating any season, it is vital to understand that whether
we participate or not, Jesus will fulfill His role and function as the One
who holds the Key of David—opening that which no man can shut
and shutting what no man can open. He is bringing justice and has-
tening righteousness in the nations.

Because David was a priest, prophet, *and* King, the Key of David
speaks of intimacy, revelation, and authority. He engaged in these
three dimensions of priestly, prophetic, and apostolic worship as the
Psalmist of Israel. We have often been concerned with *either* the
priestly, the revelatory, or governmental dimension of Heaven on
earth. Fullness demands that all three join and work together.

Out of the priestly offering, the keys of prophetic revelation are
being placed into apostolic doors in our cities and regions. In our
neighborhoods, schools, college campuses, courtrooms, and financial institutions, moments of transition are made available to us as
the apostolic church. Prophetic keys of revelation are given to us
through the prophets, prophetic worship, prophetic atmosphere, and
angelic visitation—bringing understanding from Heaven's perspective! The apostolic doors that specific revelations are to unlock will be
typically influenced and accessed by apostles.

Keys of revelation that the prophetic anointing makes available are partnering with the doors that apostolic anointing and authority are making available! The two working together are opening and closing strategic places and causing a shift. In this coming season, keys must connect to 'doors' in order for the opening and closing of strategic places.

The Key of David is being turned in the locks of our regions and cities!

PARTNERING WITH THE FIVE-FOLD

In the days ahead, Soundforgers must also integrate with and operate alongside five-fold leadership. In seeing individuals, regions, or spheres of society transformed, apostles spearhead and build according to the apostolic mandate given to them from Heaven. The other five-fold leaders are governmental equippers who work with this mission or blueprint given by God. In the local church or other sphere, this plan sets the tone and direction for all ministry and implementation. Soundforgers must be aware of, and partner with this blueprint also if they are to know which keys are being placed into which doors in their city or region.

It is accurate to say that five-fold anointings are emerging in all arenas. Whether this is found in preaching, teaching, declaration, prayer, worship, or ministry, we are required to work with all aspects of the Holy Spirit for corporate advancement and to see the release of Heaven on Earth. The partnering of five-fold governmental ministries with the ministry of the psalmist and minstrel will be a powerful force in the nations in the coming season. The increase of

Kingdom government that is being bestowed upon worship and music is mantling it with ability to propel worshipers to new levels in the Spirit. We will see increasingly that new places of His presence are easily reached in the corporate through the marrying of worship and the five-fold ministry gifts. Governing music will increasingly find itself attached to ministries through which the governing power of Christ is allowed to function. Where powerful apostolic, prophetic, evangelistic, pastoral, and teaching gifts are raised we will see Sound-forgers positioned alongside, releasing governing and governmental music. The Holy Spirit wants to move and sweep through with extreme power, causing an uprooting of apathy and delusion, distraction and inactivity. Powerful outpourings of God's presence, declarations and initiatives are being released that bring shifts across entire regional structures and social arenas.

God wants a partnering of governmental sound with governmental authority for His purpose, and Soundforgers can operate alongside five-fold leaders in many ways. Together, five-fold leaders and Soundforgers are ascending together into the presence of God, grasping Heaven's purpose for the moment and are transferring the appropriate sounds and declarations into the earth. Father's Sound-forgers are releasing sounds and songs that literally prophesy what He wants released in the corporate. These sounds and songs are resonating accurately with what apostles and prophets are sensing and seeing. The ministry functions of the five-fold and the psalmist are beginning to resonate on the same frequency with the heart of God and each other. When justice and righteousness are being sounded from Heaven, Soundforgers are resonating, reproducing, and releasing representation of this aspect of God's heart into the Earth. These sounds and declarations activate and confirm to God's governmental leaders what is already stirring within them by the Spirit of God; highlighting what He wants to unlock and break open in His Body. As governing decrees are made by leaders, a path is opened for the Body to walk upon and the apostolic Church is able to function in taking action based upon what has been revealed according to their spheres of influence and authority.

In this season it is important that Soundforgers look for and gravitate toward apostles and prophets and the apostolic mandates given to gatherings or churches. Look for apostolic and prophetic anointings that emerge in the corporate and partner with them! The operation of our anointing and gifting in isolation is not enough. Together, five-fold leaders, Soundforgers, and the whole Body of Christ are partnering with Heaven, carrying a breaker anointing to penetrate the hardest places in the Earth.

One who breaks open the way will go up before them; they will break through the gate and go out. Their King will pass through before them, the Lord at their head (Micah 2:13).

In her book *The Breaker Anointing*, Barbara Yoder says, "God is marching into the midst of our Church services; and when He shows up He will come as the triumphant Lion of the Tribe of Judah…with this release a new sound in worship is leading the way…. An aspect of apostolic worship will break out in this season and be multiplied across the nation and throughout the world. It is not the pastoral

Jesus-and-me kind of worship; rather it is the sound of triumph. It is our King, our apostolic leader, leading us."[7]

The Body of Christ is currently working through the defining of the apostle, prophet, pastor, teacher, and evangelist in terms of their practical function individually and together. How the apostle and prophet marry and work together is being particularly spotlighted right now by the Holy Spirit. Many apostles and prophets are finding themselves at crossroads in the way they relate to each other. There are potential division places over the way that they make decisions and function together within the local church. God is causing them to be *mutually dependent* upon each other—and this is new and may even be disturbing for many apostles and prophets that often operate independently of each other. There are some forerunners in the Body of Christ who have already walked out this process. However, many are facing this issue for the first time. We must be intentional in moving toward the complete fusing together of apostles and prophets and not draw back from God's intended plan.

PARTNERING WITH ANGELIC FORCES

The activity of angels is prevalent throughout Scripture and crucial to the release of God's purposes. Angelic beings appear to Abraham and Sarah, visit Sodom and Gomorrah, wrestle with Jacob and address Joshua. Zechariah the prophet has conversations with an angel during his eight visions. Angelic activity and communication were central to the unfolding of the birth of Jesus, the life of the New Testament Church and its apostles. In the New Testament alone, angelic visitation and interaction is seen over a hundred times. We cannot underestimate, or refuse to rely on the presence of angels as we move toward cooperating with the atmosphere of Heaven.

Angels are intimately acquainted with the glory of God and are involved in worshiping around the throne of God right now—thousands of them ascend and descend, moving between Heaven and earth. Just as in the vision the Lord gave me regarding the emerging Soundforgers, angels are engaged in releasing revelation of the sounds, songs, and atmosphere of Heaven into the lives of those who worship. As Heaven is opened over our lives we are given access to the songs that the angels are releasing. I have had personal encounters with angelic beings and was powerfully impacted and changed by a fresh revelation of Jesus and the atmosphere of Heaven. We do not worship them or pray to them, but we can know their presence and incredible influence—understanding that they are fully committed to establishing Heaven's rule and reign in the earth.

In aligning with God-assignments, Soundforgers partner with the angelic forces that are set over our regions and cities. It is clear from Scripture that there are both regional demonic and angelic armies (see Eph. 6:12; Rev. 2:1,12,18). In the Book of Daniel, principalities could not prevent the persistent prayers of a consecrated man, even though the answer was withheld for a short time due to war in the heavenly dimension. Similarly Soundforgers are to consistently release the sounds and songs of Heaven and wait for the final answer to come. In teaching on how we align with these heavenly allies, Kris Vallotton from Bethel Church illustrates how words that originate from Heaven will be backed by Heaven!

The Lord has established His throne in heaven, and His king-
dom rules over all. Praise the Lord, you His angels, you
mighty ones who do His bidding, who obey His word. Praise
the Lord, all His heavenly hosts, you His servants who do His
will (Psalm 103:19-21).

Angels are assigned to enforce the words and commands origi-
nating with God and not the plans or words of humanity. As we
release prophetic and apostolic worship based upon what Heaven is
declaring and decreeing (submitted underneath apostolic ministry
and their blueprint from Heaven) we secure the partnership of angels
who recognize the Word of the Lord and the true mark of authority on
our lives.

PARTNERING WITH INTERCESSION

Another angel, who had a golden censer, came and stood at
the altar. He was given much incense to offer, with the
prayers of all the saints, on the golden altar before the
throne. The smoke of the incense, together with the prayers
of the saints, went up before God from the angel's hand.
Then the angel took the censer, filled it with fire from the
altar, and hurled it on the earth… (Revelation 8:3-5).

Prayer is the hinge-place of communication with God—the
Author of revelation, declaration, and decrees. In seeing the atmosphere of Heaven released, we cannot avoid the partnership Heaven is

bringing between worship and intercession. There is such a move toward it all over the earth. It is one of the platforms in the Spirit that God is raising to maneuver the Body into the place that He ultimately desires it to be. The blending of worship and intercession is one of the forerunner settings *facilitating the progression* from priestly to prophetic worship and from the prophetic into apostolic worship. Where prayer and worship flow together for an extended time, we experience a practical meeting place of dwelling, listening and declaring. Intercession in its very nature and place as a forerunner ministry often conceives, recognizes and then draws to itself other functions in the Body that are ready for significant change. The place of intercession is a *birthing* place that *showcases* and *pre-stewards* much of what is coming to the Church and the nations. In the case of its marrying with psalmists and minstrels, I feel that this is truly the case. Revelation chapter 5 illustrates *Harp and Bowl*—the marrying of worship and intercession:

> *...the four living creatures and the twenty-four elders fell down before the Lamb. Each one had a harp and they were holding golden bowls full of incense, which are the prayers of the saints. And they sang a new song...* (Revelation 5:8-9).

The houses of prayer that are emerging all over the nations are characterized by merging priestly, prophetic and apostolic worship *with* priestly, prophetic and apostolic intercession. Rather than functioning independently, the joining of these strategic elements with those standing in the five-fold office is bringing breakthrough like never before! These houses of prayer are calling the city-wide Church to new dimensions of defensive and offensive prayer and declaration. The International House of Prayer in Kansas City, the 24/7 worldwide prayer movement, the Strategic Prayer Schools in the UK, the Justice House of Prayer in Washington D.C., along with many others internationally, have been established and called to be more than prayer meetings, more than crisis response centers, more than watches. They are birthed out of the heart of God and are forming us into a global house of prayer for all nations (see Isa. 56:7). They exist to see the land they stand upon become a place of interaction of Heaven and earth. These houses of legislation carry individual characteristics based upon their geographic location and specific assignment. Some are grassroots and others formal; some operate in disused buildings, and others meet at the seat of Civil Government. Some gather individuals around a particular injustice and others fuse people together who have redemptive authority in a particular area such as false religion. All have the same purpose—to legislate truth from Heaven into the Earth. Many of our cities are receiving a deluge of prayer from the governmental level to local schools and individuals in specific neighborhoods. Globally, there are more Christians being mobilized and released in strategic prayer than ever before. We have shifted from petition and pleading to declaration and decreeing. God is raising governmental houses of prayer that will contend with every other government and every other house of prayer that is founded upon the religions of foreign gods or the humanistic, religious power base of the compromised Church.

Soundforgers and intercessors are partnering together to see the demonstration of the Kingdom and strategic prayer is being raised over key cities and strategic gateways into our nations. They are decreeing and declaring. They are denying the authority of terror, disease, perversion, injustice and death—forbidding the rule of all that is not lawful. Terrorism and fear will not have the final word in our nations. Mercy triumphs over judgment (see James 2:13) and if we will humble ourselves, turn from our ways and pray—He promises to heal our land (see 2 Chron. 7:14). There are people in the earth who understand their position *before* the Father and their position *in* the Son. They are known in the Spirit and live to move within and to legislate the will of God—from Heaven into the earth.

> Says the Lord "I will answer the Heavens, and they shall answer the Earth. The Earth shall answer with grain, with new wine, and with oil; they shall answer Jezreel [God will sow]. Then I will sow her for Myself in the Earth, and I will have mercy on her who had not obtained mercy... (Hosea 2:21-23 NKJV).

In this passage we see a promise of the Lord to answer the Heavens. This speaks of Him responding to what has already been sown into the Heavens by us as we worship and pray. It then says that the Earth will answer with grain, new wine, and oil—which are symbols of spiritual seed, revival, and the Holy Spirit! This also results in mercy for those who have not known Him. It is necessary to see a release from Heaven to earth at the hand of God rather than to try and build from only an earthly standpoint and to see us break through into the

Heavenly.[8] The Father has done all that He intends to do through the cross and resurrection and in this age, life pours down through an *already open* Heaven. We must live from our true identity, from an Ephesians positional reality (see Eph.1:3, 2:6) declaring and legislating who He is and what His Kingdom looks like.

We understand that a merging of worship and intercession is taking place that no longer operates within an old structure. A pre-selected set of worship songs followed by a prayed list of needs is giving way to a flow that is enabling us to engage, perceive and declare from Heaven's perspective and God's heart. Prophetic and apostolic worship is not seen as a preliminary or a tag-on but an essential element in the partnership to fulfill the call. Practically, needing to see and pray from Heaven's perspective, intercessors must engage priestly intimacy and worship that enables the climb. In these times of priestly worship, individuals also have the opportunity to draw again and again from the presence of God and so receive fresh strength to pray. The cycle of prayer and worship causes there to be a focusing on the Father where specific assigned prayer can be discovered and released.

The Lord has been causing the new breed of Soundforger to be sheltered and developed within houses of prayer. They provide an ideal equipping climate for the new breed of musicians to mature and also nurture an expansion into new areas of operation and gifting. I have experienced some of my greatest times of legislative apostolic worship alongside prayer leaders, intercessors, apostles, and prophets. Many of these gatherings depended upon revelatory strategy from God and were ordered but not subject to rigid agendas, having less time constraints than other corporate settings. Elements such as strategy, sensitivity to corporate direction, understanding dimensions of the flow of the Holy Spirit, prophetic declaration, ability in targeting assignments, and deeper aspects of God's government will be added to a musician's armory and sharpened alongside intercessors.

THE SOUNDS OF THE NATIONS

I have mentioned the re-positioning of Soundforgers to significant global hot-spots for the release of Heaven's sound. Because redemptive gifts are resident in *nations and people groups as well as individuals* it is crucial that the redemptive sound in a culture or region is redeemed and given back to the Father in worship. God promises to cause righteousness and praise to spring up before every nation (see Isa. 61:11). The sound of worship from every nation and culture will be heard! Certain aspects of apostolic Heaven to earth worship can only be released by certain people groups at certain points in history. This is due to legitimate spheres of authority and geographic inheritance. It is crucial for us to partner together for true worship to be reclaimed in every created people group.

God is raising Soundforgers who will help release the sounds in the nations and unlock others that are called to transfer the sounds of Heaven into the earth. This is important to the future of governmental increase in the coming days. The activated life-message of prophetic psalmist and teacher Dan McCollum from Vacaville, California, resonates with my heart. He trains, raises up, and records indigenous prophetic psalmists as part of a missions strategy in the nations of the earth. He rightly believes that worshipers are called to be the first line of offense in recapturing the atmosphere over nations and regions. Psalmists are trained in gaining spiritual *air supremacy*—which is of course a foundational strategy of war. These initiatives carry the marks of unconventional revelatory strategy. Apostolic and prophetic implementers carry, through servant leadership, the distinguishing mark of strengthening foundations, building strategically and intentionally, and breaking the Church into new realms that God is bringing.

In the arena of praise and worship many movements have come—Australia, South Africa, the UK, and the USA can be noted for strong moves of praise and worship that have penetrated the nations as they have offered their own unique brand of worship. We have yet to see the full maturity of the sound from nations where the Church is embryonic. We have yet to hear the fullness of the sound that God has entrusted to Japan, China and the Far East, Iran, Iraq, Egypt and the Middle East, Russia and the Baltic nations, South America, Jamaica, Africa, and the Indian subcontinent. I have been actively involved in working with Iranian Christians for over a decade and had the privilege of not only leading worship for several years in an Iranian church but also encouraging indigenous songs and sounds to emerge. There is some incredibly anointed priestly, prophetic, and apostolic worship being released in the nations. We are going to not only see the revealing of the Church in the developing nations but also the sounds and song contributions that they uniquely carry to bring spiritual supremacy in our nations and governments.

PREPARATION FOR MOVES OF GOD

I believe that Second Kings 11 can be interpreted as a prophetic road sign for musicians that speaks to guarding the places of His presence—personally and geographically—in expectancy for revival.

Athaliah, the descendant of Ahab and Jezebel, destroys all of the royal heirs when she understands that her seed—and her only access to the throne—is dead. I believe this is the same demonic spirit that was operating in Jezebel as she also sought to kill and cut off the appointed and anointed of God from their inheritance (see 1 Kings 18:4). This attempt to destroy the house of David was an attack on God's redemptive plan that ultimately centered on the Messiah. However, Jehosheba (which means Jehovah has sworn, or promised) hides one of the young princes, Joash, and his nurse in the temple of the Lord for six years (see 2 Kings 11:2-3). Joash is a picture to me of God's promise to establish His Kingdom in our generation through Jesus. Jehoida, the priest, also stations protection around the prince with the commanders of the guard - making covenant with them and instructing them to "…station themselves around the king, each man with his weapons in his hand. Anyone who enters the temple must be put to death. Stay close to the king wherever he goes" (see 2 Chron. 23:7). These men are given the spears and shields that had belonged to David and faithfully protect the young heir. This speaks so clearly to me of those who have been marked by God and given the weapons of David to jealously guard His presence in these days. In the seventh year, which symbolically speaks of perfection and spiritual completeness, Joash, the young prince, is crowned and set in place (see 2 Chron. 24:1). Revival in the community breaks out as a fresh covenant is made between God and the people. The temple of Baal is torn down, its altars and idols are smashed, and all the people of the land rejoice (see 2 Kings 10:26-27).

We are coming to a day where man's self-appointed rule over the things of God, our movements and slants are giving way to an outbreak of moves of God that will see communities, whole regions, and nations affected and maneuvered into the Kingdom of God. Apostolic musicians are being prepared and repositioned for the coming moves of God as He is restructuring the ranks in this season. If you have a call to be a psalmist in the coming places of revival, you may find yourself starved and quenched. This could mean that you are in the correct place of preparation, or it may just be that there is a time of realignment coming to your life that will propel you into the place of seeing the expression of the Kingdom on earth—for that you have been praying and longing.

He is entrusting us with more in these days. It has been in the earth since a shepherd boy discovered you could have a heart after God's own heart and developed his own category of music—Tabernacle worship. David demonstrated that the Father was after the heart of His people and wanted to **be** with them, **speak through them**, and **govern** with them.

> *And in mercy shall the throne be established: and he shall sit upon it in truth in the tabernacle of David, judging, and seeking judgment, and hasting righteousness* (Isaiah 16:5 KJV).

From the blood-covered mercy seat, Jesus our Warrior-Wooer, Lion-Lamb sits in the midst of Tabernacle worship and hastens righteousness and justice in the earth.

The cry in the Spirit is: Let every anointed psalmist and minstrel begin to move in his or her anointing and authority to truly lead His Bride into the counsel chamber and out into the earth with the war cry against all that is not of Heaven. She is called to be captivated and, in turn, carry the liberating, authoritative Word of God upon her lips. Let the atmosphere of Heaven come. Let transformation in our cities and regions begin.

ENDNOTES

1.   Jennifer Miller, "The Weeping Room—Pathway to Strategy," January 2004. (Source: http://www.whitedoveministries.org/content/ArchivesItem_11_191_v, accessed 14 May 2008.)

2.   Concept taken from *Understanding the Prophetic Psalmist* by Dan McCollom, Bethel School of the Prophets Training Manual, 2006.

3.   www.andyhunter.com, accessed 14 May 2008.

4.   Synergy or synergism (from the Greek synergos, meaning working together) refers to the phenomenon in which two or more separate influences or agents acting together create an effect greater than the sum of the effects each is able to create independently.

5. Will Ford III, *Prayer for Generational Transfer*, June 4, 2006, Sojourn Church, Dallas, TX.

6. Ed Delph, *Church @ Community* (Lake Mary, FL: Creation House, 2005), 196-197.

7. Barbara J. Yoder, *The Breaker Anointing* (Ventura, CA: Regal Books, 2004), 75.

8. Dutch Sheets, Prayer Summit 2000, Prayer for the Nations, London, UK.

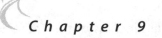

Chapter 9

Emerging Characteristics

Prophetic and apostolic Soundforgers emerging in the nations are carrying specific characteristics that mark them. By identifying different gift mixes that are emerging in Soundforgers, we will be able to correctly assign individuals to particular God objectives. It is crucial that we look at these possible marks as guideposts to recognize and nurture giftings and not as a list of requirements. Some are equipped to carry a greater deposit of intimacy and others breathe out and stir the activating fire of God. These are obviously not closed definitions but simply highlight some categories we are seeing emerge:

- ***Soaking Minstrels***

The sound emerging from some Soundforgers is primarily weighted in the area of soaking worship. Through them there is a deposit of the manifest presence of God welcomed in to a gathering or region that allows God's people to literally be saturated in the presence and peace of Heaven. Extended times of resting and waiting on God are welcomed in by psalmists that carry this anointing. The door to contemplation and revelation is opened to us through musicians

155

that understand Heaven's rest and allow dimensions of the Father's peace to inhabit and infiltrate the music they forge. Times of intentional soaking, corporately or individually, provide a necessary retreat for us in the middle of a pace of life that seeks to rob us of intimacy with God. We will see the restoration and alignment of our mind, will, and emotions as we wait. Psalm 23:1-3 is a well-known portion of Scripture and focuses upon this place of basking in the deep places of His presence:

> *The Lord is my shepherd, I shall not be in want. He makes me lie down in green pastures, he leads me beside quiet waters, he restores my soul* (Psalm 23:1-3).

I imagine that the instrumentation and tone of this song from David carried within it an anointing to impart rest, solitude, and restoration. Melodies and chord structures forged by soaking minstrels are saturated with the peace-giving, restorative nature of the Holy Spirit.

• *Intimacy Seekers*

The Father's heart is captured and communicated by some Soundforgers as they connect us back into intimacy with the Father. Their anointing is similar to those that help invite soaking worship but is different in that it activates more of a response than an abandoned resting. These psalmists often offer incredible songs of love to Him that say what we cannot always find the words to say. Like this extract from Song of Songs, they also sing and release songs of acceptance, love, and healing from the Father's heart over the Church. Partnering with inner healing, prayer, and counsel, the deepest wounding and damage can be repaired.

> *My lover spoke and said to me, "Arise my darling, my beautiful one, and come with me. See! The winter is past; the rains are over and gone* (Song of Solomon 2:10-11).

- *River Releasers*

River releasers are used to call the Body into refreshing and joy. Reminding us of the life-giving aspects of God they intuitively flow in and out of the moving of the Spirit of God. These Soundforgers locate and lock into the joy of Heaven; pulling it down and releasing it into the earth realm. The fruit of heaviness, battle weariness, oppression, and ungodly burden-bearing is broken off when we flow with these minstrels in the river. They release a necessary dimension of Heaven into our worship experience that balances the seasons of engaging in war and intensity.

> *There is a river whose streams make glad the city of God, the holy place where the Most High dwells* (Psalm 46:4).

- *Breakers*

Some Soundforgers carry the breaker anointing as a characteristic of their music and sound. They carry an anointing that causes a sudden and dynamic awakening and are often used to break and propel corporate groups into the next dimension of what God has for them. Apathy, passivity, distraction, deception, introspection, and anything that keeps Heaven carriers diminished is a target for these breakers. They are often uniquely aware of the strategy of the enemy to oppress the Church and focus upon a specific area to target in the context of worship. Their sound has an inbuilt anointing to demolish enemy fortifications and enlarge the people of God.

> *He is the God who avenges me, who subdues nations under me, who saves me from my enemies* (Psalm 18:47-48).

- ### *Governmental Psalmists*

Certain musicians are being set over specific governmental gates and regions. Their sound is equipped with the ruling anointing of God, and they are enabled to release sounds and declarations that set a watch over dimensions of human government and decision making. These particular Soundforgers may be more aware of their assigned geographic sphere of influence than other Kingdom musicians. Just as prophets operate in a region, these Soundforgers carry the heart of Heaven for righteousness and justice in the realm of civil government and are used to operate in the realm of the Spirit to bring change and raise Heaven's plumb line. They often partner with houses of prayer.

> *Lift up your heads, O you gates; be lifted up, you ancient doors, that the King of glory may come in* (Psalm 24:7).

This song speaks to spiritual gates which are symbolically places of authority.

- ***Fire Stirrers***

Fire stirrers carry music that re-lights the fire of passion in God's people. They release fresh fuel onto a flame that has become diminished and stir fresh fire in the corporate. These Psalmists bring an atmosphere where fresh anointing and gift re-activation are released. They are used to refresh the desire to run with God in His purposes and release new passion for the headlines of God. Our place, purpose, and destiny as a people are promoted back to the forefront through these lead worshipers.

> *What god is so great as our God? You are the God who performs miracles; you display your power among the peoples* (Psalm 77:13-14).

- ***Intercessory Psalmists***

Intercessory psalmists partner with prayer and live to release a cry from the earth for change. They carry assignments from the Holy Spirit that are released in musical intercession. Extended waiting and watching to catch the heart of God, working with intercession, forming prayer songs, helping intercessors to climb, align with God and receive revelation characterize these Soundforgers. We see intercessory psalmists functioning in the book of Psalms, as many of the Psalms were actually sung prayers.

> *Help us, O God our Savior, for the glory of your name....Why should the nations say, "Where is their God?"* (Psalm 79:9-10).

- ### *Issachar Psalmists*

These Soundforgers have understanding of the times and perceive what to do. From the perspective of the now of God these psalmists have the most accurate and pointed prophetic anointing.

> *These are the numbers of the men armed for battle who came to David at Hebron to turn Saul's kingdom over to him, as the LORD had said:...men of Issachar, who understood the times and knew what Israel should do—200 chiefs, with all their relatives under their command* (1 Chronicles 12:23,32).

They are able to see clearly where a church, ministry or region is right now within the plan of God and will craft prophetic and apostolic worship around this reality. Their primary motivation will be to see the Holy Spirit reveal current spiritual location and help move the corporate into the next step as God allows.

Soundforgers may move in one or several of these dimensions in a worship setting or may exclusively operate in one consistently as a mark of their ministry. Some from this list do lend themselves more obviously to one of the dimensions of priestly, prophetic, or apostolic worship. The specific anointings of the five-fold offices also help us locate as usual. For example, those who lead us into soaking and intimacy will probably be operating out of a pastoral anointing more than any of the others. Our purpose is to become available to operate in any of the five-fold anointings and focuses, while also embracing any of the three strands of priestly, prophetic or apostolic worship as the Holy Spirit releases.

GENERAL BRANDING

Some general branding that we are seeing in the lives of Sound-forgers include:

Living as a worshiper:
- Engages a lifestyle of honoring His presence rooted as an integral part of life
- Honors the passionate pursuit of His presence

Is familiar with the Bridal identity of the Church:
- Leads worship out of the presence of God, welcoming the Bride
- Loves the Bride as a friend of the Bridegroom

Engages in priestly, prophetic, and apostolic dimensions of worship:
- Is listening for the now sound of Heaven
- Is familiar with the priestly and esteems intimacy with Jesus
- Draws on the revelatory and releases prophetic worship
- Demonstrates a level of breakthrough in worship that is apostolic in content, strategy, and authority
- Moves in a warfare and breaker anointing like David
- As a worshiper of God, will always be led to devastate the plans of the enemy

Understands the Father revealed as the Master of Break-through (2 Sam. 5:20):

- Has an ability to locate and partner with corporate anointings and with other ministries
- Partners with and submits to five-fold leaders
- Is a strategist who knows the Master strategist
- Searches for and aligns with the revealed will of God in corporate moments
- Puts corporate purpose and strategy above personal ministry agenda
- Is geographically and assignment sensitized
- Desires to re-dig the spiritual wells of the previous generations

Understands spheres of authority in different settings:

- Aware of the sphere of influence given to them by God and released to them by their Senior leaders
- Understands moving within authority by association in certain settings
- Aware of "authority for the moment" as they are released by five-fold leaders

Is able to perceive and move directionally where given authority to do so:

- Engages their revelatory gifting in the corporate
- Sure of the voice of God to align with purpose in worship

- Unstoppable in courage to move with God when sent and released on assignment

Understands the realm of declaration:
- Engages in personal declaration over their personal lives and family
- Engages in corporate declaration over their churches and local sphere of influence
- Partners with the local and city-wide church in making declarations over their city and region
- Develops new songs out of apostles' and prophets' decrees

SPECIFIC EXPRESSIONS OF APOSTOLIC AND PROPHETIC WORSHIP AND MUSIC

As these Kingdom musicians emerge, we need to be prepared for some specific expressions of prophetic and apostolic worship:

- Revelatory prophetic or governing apostolic songs and declarations in the context of worship leading.

- Spontaneous response songs working behind and alongside apostles and prophets in a corporate gathering including forging songs that pick up aspects, specific concepts, or phrases of their decrees and declarations for the corporate to sing.

- Pre-written prophetic and apostolic songs that are not spontaneous but that come out of the current flow of direction in the Church. They speak to areas of important focus for the Body and are being sung by local or regional church congregations for a season. These will be used by God to help shift the Church into the next place of alignment in specific areas.

- Prophetic and apostolic sounds and music that prompt a shift in the room or in the spirit realm over a region. These sounds inspired by the Holy Spirit will stir apostles and prophets to declare as with Elisha in Second Kings 3:14.

According to the apostle John's encounter with Heaven and the throne of God in the Book of Revelation, the four living creatures around the throne cry out day and night:

Holy, holy, holy is the Lord God Almighty, who was, and is, and is to come (Revelation 4:7-9).

He exists eternally in the past, present, and future realms and so priestly, prophetic and apostolic songs can exist in one of these dimensions: **The Past**—reaching back and highlighting redemptive purpose and history. **The Present**—in sync with the now of God. **The Future**—releasing a declaration of Heaven's will and purpose ahead of the circumstance, breaking in before we arrive.

For example, a **priestly** earth to Heaven song could be (a) focused on praying for an ancient well of renewal to be opened in a geographic area, (b) be extravagantly thankful for the refreshing we see presently or (c) thank him for His faithfulness in the future increase of His Kingdom in that region. Prophetic and apostolic worship would obviously have different content and focus.

GOD'S LEFT-HANDERS

God loves unconventional people. Biblically, a left-handed warrior was considered inferior to a right-handed one. In the opening chapters of Judges, we see Ehud, a left-handed warrior who went unconventionally into the enemy's private room and with a message delivered a sword through to his backbone (see Judges 3:20-22). Many of the deliverers that God raised up for Israel's ultimate good were left-handers—unconventional in their approach or background. Other unconventional warriors in this passage are Shamgar, who struck down 600 with an ox goad; Deborah, a woman without whom Barak will not go to war; and Gideon, who played hide and seek in the family wine press before going to war with only 300 men. (See Judges chapters 3-6.) Many emerging Soundforgers are left-handers— engaging creativity that is capturing a generation.

Although many formulas are in place that define successful praise and worship, professionalism, incredible arrangements, choirs and multimedia presentations are all secondary to the participation with the "now" of God in the corporate. In a church culture often disabled by diminished creativity, we are plagued by the status quo—

reproducing dull and passionless replicas rather than reckless follow-
ers of Jesus, who calls us to risk all and die. This in no way gives us an
excuse to be deliberately mysterious or misunderstood out of our
unhealed places, but it is clear that God's chosen do not always follow
a normal accepted route in walking out God's intent in their lives. Like
God's left-handers, Soundforgers are called into an equal uniqueness.
They are made to partner with the Deliverer and infuse the earth with
only what is lawful in Heaven. Soundforgers are being given creative
license, tradition-deconstructing liberty and penetrating permission
by the One whose utter surrender paid for the arenas of society and
nations where He is sending us.

ESTHER GENERATION

Esther's God-journey provides understanding on the characteristics of emerging Soundforgers. Captured by an enemy strategy in the
middle of a God assignment, Esther responds in extravagant consecration—prepares herself—and pursues Heaven for the final word.
The Esther generation is now rising out of the place of preparation in
specific regions. At such a time as this a separated generation can
stand as the Bride in the priestly dimension before the King and turn
the decree of the enemy with the decree of God.

While we are waiting in the secret place of intimacy secure in the
love of the Bridegroom, captivated by His beauty—both His heart
and governmental rule will be sensed and apostolic declarations will
be formed and released.

In the unfolding of Esther's assignment, Mordecai, as a picture of the Church, is vindicated. The key principle in understanding the emergence of apostolic declaration is that the King calls for them to write their own decree (see Esther 8:8) that displaces the decree of Haman.[1] Out of the place of seeing His scepter of personal favor released, the Esther generation is emerging to decree apostolically in the name of the King over the Earth.

Esther—you are called to prepare, approach, and legislate.

ENDNOTE

1.   It is interesting that Haman the Agagite only existed because God's people did not fully obey previous mandates from the Lord to pursue and wipe out their enemy in a previous generation. (See Exodus 17:8-16.)

Chapter 10

Unlocking Emerging Worship

The previous chapters have been weighted on theory and releasing identity. I hope that you have a greater grasp of what God is doing in the earth through emerging worship and see a clearer vision of what you, or a Soundforger you know, was designed and created for. As we function as prophetic and apostolic worship teams, information and equipment to help move us from the *why* into the *how* is crucial. This chapter focuses on some steps to unlock us practically in a new dimension.

REVELATION 101

Knowing that revelation provides the building blocks for prophetic and apostolic worship, how do we cultivate a life that is sensitized to hearing words from God? Are there practical ways to live a life that is receptive to revelation? Here are some foundations:

- Spend adequate time with Him. Allow your relationship with Jesus to become the most treasured thing in your life. Feed yourself constantly on the Word of God. He can release a *rhema* or *now* word of God to us from Scripture as we deposit His written word in us. Allow your ear to become open to these "now" passages of Scripture He gives you and also harvest what the Spirit of God is saying to your church and to the wider Body of Christ though His apostles and prophets.

- Develop intimacy with the Holy Spirit. Become sensitized to His presence and ways. As you listen for the voice of the Holy Spirit—ask, expect, and wait. Demystify revelation in your thinking. Adam walked in simple, unbroken communication with God before the Fall, and we have been restored to that former reality as sons and daughters. It is as simple as listening for and responding to your father's voice. Allow the Holy Spirit to teach and reveal to you the mood of Heaven regarding various circumstances. Be open to all of the ways He might communicate with you. Look for the language of the Holy Spirit. He speaks through Scripture, dreams, visions, impressions, your senses, creation, billboards, MySpace, blogs, friends, or leaders.

- Daily submit your mind, will, and emotions to God. Eagerly desire and seek to move prophetically (see 1 Cor. 14:1).

- Inquire of the Lord like David. No one inquired and sought after Heaven like this man after God's heart. We see so many times in Scripture how the Father answered him and revealed exactly what he should do (see 1 Sam. 30:7, 2 Sam. 5:17-20, 2 Sam. 21:1).

- Receive training and activation in the prophetic through books, conferences, and teaching. Spend time with healthy recognized leaders that hear God's voice more clearly than you do and seek to learn from them. Allow them to help you test any revelation that you receive. Become a life-long student in learning how to communicate God's heart in a way that brings His intended life and purpose.

- Journal thoughts, Scriptures, dreams, visions, impressions, and headlines and begin to piece together the thoughts and heart of God for your sphere of influence (see Hab. 2:2).

- Test everything against the written Word of God.

DECLARATION 101

Because declaration is one of the obvious keys in releasing the revelation we receive, we can position ourselves to grow and increase. Some practical points are:

- Begin to declare truth from Scripture. Find New Testament passages that speak of who you are in Christ and begin to use them as declarations over your life. Find your voice in saying what Scripture says about you.

- Practice making declarations out loud based upon God's revealed or prophetic word to you. Enforce the reality of these truths over your past, present, and future.

- Begin making Godly declarations over your family and every sphere where you have been given authority.

- Begin to sing out passages of Psalms. Allow the Holy Spirit to inspire and teach you how to move in the three realms of the priestly, prophetic, and apostolic.

- Include any revelation you receive into these Psalms and develop spontaneous songs that are prophetic or apostolic—outward in their DNA.

INCLUDING THE REVELATORY AND APOSTOLIC IN CORPORATE WORSHIP

In successfully including what we hear from God into a corporate worship set, I have discovered that pre-situation prayer over a worship time greatly increases my perception of what God is saying. I will often pray ahead of time and sometimes fast for a particular worship set. This allows me to align with both the *what* and *how* of God's heart. Is the Holy Spirit revealing a pastoral *father's heart* moment? Or is there a sense that He wants to move the corporate into fighting for their destiny? Where is this particular church or city in its destiny timeline from Heaven's perspective? Is there a *now* parable that Jesus is speaking to the generation I am leading? What headlines is He giving me? What Scriptures? I often write down the revelation I receive.

Alongside my song lists, these thoughts, pictures, Scriptures, phrases, and concepts become the building material for prophetic and apostolic worship. The Holy Spirit might reveal a very specific word or only a general sense of what He wants to do. I will also *practice* the prophetic as I prepare—forging songs, chord progressions, and musical phrases that *speak* into what I know to be the unveiling of God's heart. I also position myself outwardly and make sure that I am spiritually free to make the declarations that He is making—checking that the overflow of my heart is not restricted through unforgiveness, unbelief, or worry, for example. I *find my voice* and the full measure of authority that He has handed to me.

As you move into leading worship, be open to include the revelation you have received. This could be in the form of singing, speaking, praying, prophesying, or declaring. It is necessary to draw people into a priestly devotional focus through relevant themes, prayer and Scriptures—but we are called to unlock prophetic and apostolic worship. Begin to practice moving in and out of all three dimensions of worship when alone or with your teams. Be expectant to share beyond just a *devotional* focus into where God is shifting and moving the group you are leading.

It is not necessary to include everything we received in advance into a worship set. It usually becomes apparent quite quickly which direction the Holy Spirit is moving. God often speaks through other leaders that are gathered, so be prepared to pick up on any prayers, revelation, or Scriptures shared by others. Look for prophetic signposts. Also, stay open to the spontaneous—much of our revelation can come suddenly through the inspiration of the Holy Spirit as we lead, causing us to speak and release words and concepts that we had not previously thought of or been focused upon. At times you may sense there is something God is wanting to do—but not be exactly sure what it is. Is He bringing a pastoral anointing? Warfare? Soaking? Outward declaration over the city? Did someone leading in prayer transition into something that you felt was on God's heart? Did a leader clearly interject a change in direction? Acknowledging to yourself and team that there is a crossroads opportunity is crucial; stay on the current song until you get clarity or simply begin to shift musically along the lines of what you are sensing and hearing. Be open to the mode and content of what He would have you share next. Just move step by step. A simple way of testing the water is to place a prophetic phrase or apostolic declaration within a worship song you are leading. You can easily pick back up on the previous song when you have released what you were carrying.

Another important factor is developing your ability to stay focused and concentrate upon hearing God. Try and become accomplished and familiar with chord progressions and lyrics so that you can flow on *auto pilot* when leading songs. This enables you to have one ear attentive to the Holy Spirit. It is a skill that takes time to develop. We have received the mind of Christ (see 1 Cor. 2:16) and can train ourselves to remain focused and intentional.

Finally, recognize who you *are* and who you are *not* as you begin to release prophetic and apostolic worship. If you are used primarily to draw people into intimacy, allow yourself to be stretched by the Holy Spirit but do not feel pressure to strive to be a fire-stirring psalmist.

STEPS TO STEPPING OUT

Let's look a little more deeply into actually stepping out and releasing prophetic and apostolic worship. I am primarily speaking to vocalists here, although some of these concepts apply to musicians forging prophetic and apostolic sounds also.

A common question psalmists often ask me is, how do you know what you are carrying in the moment is from God? We first need to examine why we are feeling compelled to step out. Is the Holy Spirit developing a thought that will just not leave? Are you sensing His heart for something that He wants to communicate? Is there a theme developing, and you have a piece of the picture to contribute? Second, checking that the content lines up with the spirit of the moment is crucial. You want to make sure that content flows with what has been released so far. Are we in a priestly, prophetic, or apostolic worship dimension? Is what I want to release consistent both with Scripture and God's character? Third, what are the communication tools that enable the leader to know you are holding something that could be released? Your relationship with God, your team, and any personal pre-worship preparation will sensitize you to answer these questions.

It usually requires faith to step out. The Word says that we prophesy according to our faith (see Rom.12:6). Do you have faith to step out or are you presuming? What you are receiving spontaneously will often depend on how He normally speaks to you. Do you often hear His voice audibly? Does He often place Scripture on your heart? Do you see pictures or visions? The revelatory realm can manifest itself in different ways: at times we sense or know; sometimes we are enlarged in the seer dimension, seeing images, visions, and pictures; and sometimes we clearly hear the voice of the Holy Spirit. We can also be reminded of a Scripture or just simply know what to do because of the deposit of God's wisdom and Word in our lives. If you are not experienced at stepping out, you can always begin by singing directly out of Scripture. A certain phrase may become highlighted to you as you continue, and a theme may develop. Remember—revelation like this provides building blocks that help us form declarations.

A particular theme or focus can often become clear during an extended revelatory worship set. Whether introduced by five-fold leaders, prayer leaders or other vocalists—be committed to partnering with their content. The sign of an emerging theme is a good indicator that God is highlighting something for us. If you are sensing apostolic declaration—aim for single phrases at first that the corporate can easily pick up and sing. Develop simple repetitive melodies and rhythms. Other team vocalists can support these declarations when they surface to add momentum and strength. When working together, make room for each other and lean into a desire for corporate success—support with harmony or response phrases as others step out. Moving into prophetic and apostolic worship is not a competition to see who is carrying the most revelation—it is a vehicle for achieving corporate purpose. You may only contribute once in a worship set, but it may be the word from Heaven that shifts the corporate in a profound way. We really learn through experience and in relationship with those who are more experienced so do not be afraid of missing God or making mistakes if you have adequately allowed the Holy Spirit to prepare a right heart motive. It requires maturity to hold revelation we have received lightly, yet remain constantly open to include it.

In prophetic or apostolic worship, ultimate responsibility lies with the worship leader on the appropriate timing to release what the Lord is saying. The key word here is *responsibility*. Leaders are often more sensitized to know transition places because they have been given an area of stewardship. As a vocalist, you have to know if the worship leader has released you to act independently in contributing new revelation. During a worship set, where several vocalists are contributing to a theme in rapid fire, this is not the time to require that each one check in with the worship leader before singing out. I usually require this from vocalists when there is a clear crossroads place, and when they are going to change the focus of what the corporate is experiencing. If what you are going to sing, share, or pray changes the direction of the gathering, be extra sensitive to timing and know if you need to communicate with the worship leader. For example, prophesying *strength* when we are in an intimate moment, or moving into apostolic declaration. Be careful not to repeat what has already been shared unless the worship leader makes it clear that the Holy Spirit is returning there. If the flow of content has *moved on* already, you may need to move on also, or wait for another opportunity to step out. As a leader, I just need to be sure that what a vocalist sings out is going to consistent with the direction that I am sensing, or if not, that they have an appropriate platform to support them as they present what God is saying. If you are a vocalist waiting to release a war cry—and the sound or content is primarily pastoral—wait for the sound of war to be affirmed and set up by the worship leader or musicians. This is a team sport. I have discovered that the Holy Spirit is more concerned about the gathering achieving its purpose than we are!

TEAM DYNAMICS

Working with at least one other person means you already have a team and this requires navigating through team dynamics! Start by teaching and equipping teams to distinguish between and maneuver through priestly, prophetic, and apostolic worship. When working with teams, based upon your briefing and understanding, explain the boundaries you are to work within in specific gatherings. Communicating to them ahead of time which worship sets give opportunity to each of these will produce expectation, clarity, and unity as you begin to move in a particular direction as a leader. Clearly communicate ahead of time what you require of them and how *you* particularly flow with God. Build in ways to communicate if any team members have revelatory or apostolic input during a worship set. Making it clear that you are submitted to and tracking with other leadership will also reinforce confidence as they support you.

Remember that psalmists are called to carry and release the atmosphere of Heaven. We expect miracles, breakthrough, enlarging, joy, life, and strength because He is all of these things. Train musicians to play intuitively and remain sensitive to what Heaven is doing during a worship set. Consistently providing feedback during rehearsals and after worship sets to illustrate where we partnered with God and where we did not builds a team's ability to locate and respond. Intentionally communicate in ways that enlarge your musicians' ability to discern what is happening or happened in the realm of the *spirit*—not just the realm of *music*. Release musicians, in appropriate settings, to have freedom to forge sounds that prompt, sounds that build, sounds that declare—and affirm when a sound is marked with the *now* of God.

It is also helpful to develop musical systems that enable you to flow and transition from one place to another during a worship set. Musically setting up opportunities to change direction is crucial. Changing feel or intensity and communicating which instruments can or should initiate this is important. Developing simple chord progressions that repeat, or using part of a song already in the set can provide a background for overlaying prophetic and apostolic worship. Develop a culture among teams where they are ready to move direction at any moment. Developing communication signals that work for you in worship sets and building inter-team relationships and trust will help teams transition when the Holy Spirit is transitioning.

It is also helpful to be aware of the hidden potential, current limitations, and maturity level of those who serve with us. Know the character and calling of those you run with. I mentioned earlier about working with vocalists in *grassroots* prophetic development. In these settings we can practice the prophetic in a non-platform environment and provide adequate feedback and mentoring. Watch for emerging prophetic gifting and ask them what revelation they have received or what they are sensing directionally or in the realm of the Spirit. This increases our knowledge of what God is doing in our teams and gives us understanding of our group gifting and our *available weapons base* as we navigate through ministry places.

MAKING IT WORK IN THE LOCAL CHURCH

Throughout this book we have focused on the changes taking place in different types of corporate gatherings; however, most Soundforgers operate primarily within the local church. This is the venue that concerns them—their primary place of ministry function. There are several major hinge factors in successfully leveraging into new aspects of priestly, prophetic and apostolic worship in a local setting. As this is a practical chapter, let's take a look at adequately understanding leadership function, knowing our sphere of operation and working with interlocking relationships.

As a Soundforger within the local church it helps to define our leadership relationships clearly. What I mean by this is, who am I submitted and accountable to when I lead worship? Who has responsibility in each setting where I minister? This is important because relationships are the context in which our ministry parameters are defined and walked out.

Second, we must understand the distinct purpose of each specific gathering. Corporate times have predetermined purpose and intention and we should lock into the mandate that the Holy Spirit is *writing* over the meeting. God is clear in His purpose when the church gathers together, and most leaders are very intentional about what they initiate or avoid in a specific gathering. If we grasp understanding that our times together have different functions in the Kingdom and then soundforge accordingly, we will appropriately move into Heaven's agenda on the earth in whatever setting we find ourselves. Our worship leading will be colored by our primary gift mix, but whether we lead worship in a Sunday service, a small group, or alongside intercession—we should always lend ourselves to the revealed purpose of God and leadership. We have three main corporate gatherings currently operating at our home base. Each of them is distinct and requires a different approach and awareness from me as a Soundforger. Our regular weekend services, monthly nights of worship, and our prayer-watches focus on different aspects of the Holy Spirit's ministry and function. As a leadership, our desired outcome for each gathering is completely different as they each support a different facet of our "church" life. The Holy Spirit is incredible at orchestrating, and through a combination of seeking God, pre-preparation and spontaneous response in partnership with each other, He accomplishes what He intends to accomplish.

Third, as a Soundforger, we must know the parameters within which we have permission to operate directionally. What is our given level of authority to bring a change in direction to the gathering we are leading? Fourthly, linked with this, we must know if we are released to include revelatory content or declarations into the worship we are leading. Is our church ready for prophetic and apostolic dimensions of worship? If so, to what degree and in which setting? Are we personally ready for the increased responsibility that this will bring? I am one of seven functioning pastors at our home base church. This gives me a peer-level authority among these leaders, but there is a level of senior leadership that I submit to in regard to corporate direction and revelation.

Another factor to consider is that sometimes the *congregation* we are leading may be ready for increased parameters in worship but we *personally* may not be. It is crucial to wait for the promotion of the Lord. Permission from our leaders to release revelation or a directional word or song is usually determined by several factors: our calling, character, maturity level, ability to walk out the consequences of missing God, the need to be right, the need to be in control, the level of humility, the level of accuracy and consistency in correct interpretation of revelation. Mary Forsythe, president of Kingdom Living Ministries in Dallas, Texas, often teaches that, "The Holy Spirit delights to give us revelation, but we must know how to handle it. Receiving revelation is not a sign of spiritual authority or spiritual maturity; and the fact that we receive revelation does not mean we have permission to share it with others." A good safety barrier for us is—just because we have received revelation does not give us permission to share, does not mean we have the maturity to share correctly, and it does not mean that this is the time and place to share it. In regard to revelation and providing direction, we may be released by our local church leadership in one particular ministry setting but not in another. This comes under the category of staying within our assigned spheres and locking into the apostolic mission of a church.

A healthy local church will have a broad Kingdom perspective and be open to the Kingdom mandates we talked about earlier. However, churches may experience a stronger anointing in one particular ministry area, (for example, in evangelism or physical healing) or can be given authority over a particular *gate* or geographic region. This will cause a greater receptivity to prophetic revelation or apostolic declarations in this specific *weighted* area. This can help us flow with the current move in the house; or, if we are not listening or bold enough, prevent us from breaking into new arenas because we will default to the most well-trodden route—the path of least resistance.

Recently, while leading worship during our 7-11 prayer watch, I literally sensed a sharp breakthrough anointing of the Holy Spirit in the room to literally shift people into a new season. It came in quickly and there was urgency in my spirit to harvest what God was doing in the moment. I prophesied what I felt the Holy Spirit was saying and then stepped out into declaring and singing the shift over the congregation. Other leaders picked up on this theme, and it became a significant part of what God wanted to do in that setting. At other times a heartfelt and simple priestly prayer has been the catalyst that God has used to bring dramatic shift to the course of our congregation. I have seen many prophetic promptings caught and expanded upon in this way, ending with an apostolic element to cause the revelation God was bringing to become a reality. Within our specified boundaries, we can release prophetic themes and wait to see if this is confirmed and picked up by other ministry or prayer leaders. Working in teams like this will help us know how much to continue in a particular vein that we are perceiving. I later checked with my senior leader to see if I had stepped over my given boundary and scope of authority. He reassured me that there was adequate relationship built within my three years of being on staff to step out in this. Once we build relationships, we do not need to clarify our boundaries on a daily basis. We gain and develop trust with our leaders and with our churches. From time to time, parameters will need to be redefined as the church's season changes and as the strength and visibility of our personal gifting emerges. Some of the revelatory content that I receive can be communicated to my senior leaders pre-gathering and can be weighed. It does not all have to be included spontaneously in a worship set.

I wanted to highlight some of these points because, in reflection, some of my most difficult platform places have been a result of underdeveloped relationships or because of a lack of initial communication as to expectations or specific boundaries. Openly discussing the progression of a church in praise and worship will give you and leadership understanding of the potential place of priestly, prophetic, and apostolic worship in the life of your church. We have discovered that spontaneous prophetic worship emerges more successfully at first in small groups of intercessors who are more familiar with flowing with the leading of the Holy Spirit. At our base, this developed into the 7-11 prayer watch I mentioned—where we are now seeing legitimate expressions of apostolic declaration and decree over our city. Some Sunday services require us to lead a set of worship where the only revelatory input we should bring is a Spirit-led prayer or the sharing of *now* Scripture. In some settings, leadership releases me to make declarations that echo a previous decree or declaration from a five-fold leader. At other times, such as Nights of Worship and the 7-11 prayer watch, our teams have a four-hour window in which to move directionally, prophesy, declare, and navigate—where what is released in prophetic and apostolic worship is a crucial element in guiding the direction and apostolic purpose of the gathering. It's obviously crucial to know which meeting is which ahead of time! Remember that releasing prophetic revelation or apostolic declaration in worship will ultimately change the direction of the corporate gathering. If we miss the timing or content, the gathering will be shifted out of alignment, and someone with responsibility will have to clean up and get things back on track! This may not be disastrous, and the local church *is* a training ground for us to make mistakes; however, we are in a season of cultivating greater accuracy and alignment with the specifics of the Spirit. It is also crucial to communicate when we do not have any revelation or direction to bring to the table. Equally important as being released to break boundaries and move the church into new dimensions is the necessity to know when you simply do not have it. Resist being pressured to move where the Holy Spirit is not leading you. I have sometimes had to release myself from well-meaning, but strong leadership whose expectation for me to take the gathering into the third Heaven was not matching the level of revelation or anointing I was experiencing in the moment.

With answers to the above questions in place, we can navigate and lead teams with a degree of confidence while still leaning into our gifting and any anointings that emerge—knowing that we are working in partnership with local Church leadership and not against it.

ESTABLISHING A PERSONAL AUTHORITY BASE

As we focus upon practically recovering the mandate for apostolic and prophetic worship, new aspects of anointing will require new dimensions of personal responsibility and obedience in our lives. Musicians and worshipers can be susceptible to demonic strategies in specific areas. We need to grasp the keys that will enable growth in *personal* authority and therefore the *corporate* authority we have talked about in previous chapters. We need to establish and maintain what I call a personal authority base.

Engaging in prophetic and apostolic worship, we can unknowingly attempt to infiltrate spiritual territory in areas that we personally do not have authority over. Jesus stated that the enemy had nothing in Him; speaking to the truth that there was no 'landing strip' for the enemy in His own life. Unfortunately, what we do or say in secret is eventually made known in the spiritual and natural. It's a Kingdom principal (see Matt.10:26). It is not that God is out to expose our deepest sin, but if we insist on walking in a hidden addiction to something, we *will* carry the atmosphere of this with us wherever we go. It will shape our worship, relationships, speech, authority, and ultimately, our destiny. We need to know that right standing with God comes only through the blood of Jesus, and we do not have to live in fear that our places of temptation are bigger than God's plan to transform regions. But because of the way God wants to use them, Soundforgers need to live in freedom from habitual sin strongholds.

GEOGRAPHIC OPPOSITION

Spiritual forces and powers operating over cities and geographic regions (see Eph. 6:12) influence the spiritual atmosphere in particular ways that affect us personally. We have to be diligent to recognize and respond correctly to outside influence and be trained by the Holy Spirit to live above it. In my home city of Dallas, Texas, pride and independence are part of the spiritual fabric. Dallas is an affluent city, in a state that reserves the right to this day to be independent from the Constitution and the rest of the United States. Living in this spiritual atmosphere requires a consistent walk in the opposite spirit of humility and interdependence because I want to walk in a Christ-like way in the earth and have legitimate, overcoming authority in the city. Operating in the fruit of the Holy Spirit safeguards us against opening doors to wrong influence (see Gal. 5:16-19, 22-26). You know as well as I do that it is difficult to remain loving on the days when your coffee is not fixed correctly at the drive thru! But seriously, when we live and work in a particular geographic area, it may be more difficult than usual to move against the flow of the spiritual culture in one or more specific areas of life. Not all geographic regions will carry a sense of a prevailing spirit, but it is necessary to be sensitized to influence from outside spiritual sources.

In understanding and maintaining a personal authority base we should be aware of key spirits that will attempt to oppress us as Soundforgers (and can exist geographically), that seek to keep us from moving into God's purposes.

The Religious Spirit

The religious spirit manifests itself in various ways—often jealous, like the older brother of the prodigal (see Luke 15:25-31). Or alternatively—bound to the law displaying diminished grace, mercy or compassion like the Pharisees. (See Matt. 12:9-15; Luke 7:36-50; John 8:1-12.)

The religious spirit expertly takes advantage of the realm of *works* and *traditions*, keeping us substituting relationship with God and His power for a powerless existence full of empty rituals. It attempts to raise law above grace, maneuvering us into the understanding that we are able to draw near to God because of what we do rather than on the basis of Jesus' righteousness applied to our lives. This spirit hinders the full revelation of the grace of God and lures us into eating from the Tree of the Knowledge of Good and Evil, as Adam and Eve did in the Garden. This temptation is based on a lie because we already have everything we need and are fully accepted. We cannot get any more secure than in our position in Christ as a Son and joint heir. The religious spirit seeks to elevate man's work above God's— where doing things *for* Him to gain *approval* is esteemed above living from a place of complete acceptance. Condemning others for lack of works or religious activity, this spirit often performs to impress man and earthly Kingdoms, while openly judging those it perceives as weak. It often displays great zeal for the things of God and those influenced will not always join something that they consider less than perfect. Anything that is perceived to be immature or lacking will not be tolerated and perfectionism will be allowed to take the place of grace-enabled excellence. Ultimately, giving into the religious spirit leads to ever increasing pride rather than true humility.

The religious spirit often causes people to presume that God has the same opinions as them and will motivate a tearing down of all that is *wrong*. Ultimately, we end up interpreting God's plan through our traditions rather than seeing from His perspective. The religious spirit will cause us to want to live in the past rather than the present, causing us to only embrace what is safe. Other fruit in the lives of those giving themselves to a religious spirit will be a masked superiority that often makes comparisons and manifests in fault finding and criticism. This brings condemnation and guilt in those it touches rather than conviction with a door for restoration. Healthy communication and relationship will be avoided in favor of gathering alliances around false agreement.

The religious spirit influences people to believe that God cannot be released from their specific interpretation of how He works and moves. Prophetic and creatively gifted people are a prime target—simply because they operate *outside of the box* most of the time! This is a battle that Jesus fought and we will continually fight in coming days and seasons. In Second Kings 11, the rebellious Athaliah murders the true royal seed because her offspring has been rejected (see 2 Kings 11:1). Her cry is, *"treason"* when the real heir is revealed and set in place (see 2 Kings 11:13-14). Traditions of men will always cry treason when the truth of God is manifested—accusing of a departure from their form of tradition. As the Lord increasingly reveals Himself and puts His sceptre down in geographic regions, the religious will manifest in outcry.

Whether we are Soundforgers or those who love them, we can guard against the religious spirit by seeking to develop a hidden relationship with the Lord that is stronger and deeper than anything that may be publicly revealed or noticed by man. In developing a place for the Love of the Father to live in and through us, our desire for religious duty will grow dim and its pull on our lives insignificant. In seeking to hear His voice every day, turning away from dead works and traditions, and consistently strengthening ourselves in the love of God, we will become resilient to the influence of this anointing killer.[1]

Rejection

The spirit of rejection ministers a sense of unworthiness, leaving people feeling unacceptable to others and especially to God. Some of the fruit of a *root* of rejection can be: shame, identity crisis, self rejection, inferiority, anger, rejecting others before they can reject you, withdrawal, or rebellion. Rejection manifests in the inability to give or receive real meaningful love. It can ravage people, leaving them disconnected from God and other people. Unhealed wounds can give a place of authority to this demonic spirit. Rejection can be generational or ancestral—as the sins of the fathers can clearly affect us to the third and fourth generation in a family line (see Exodus 34:7). It is important for lead-worshipers to be totally healed and free from the influence of rejection. As we have already touched upon, receiving the love of the Father and living in revelation knowledge of our identity in Christ are two major foundation stones. If these are not in place we will approach everything we do from a place of being driven by insecurity and the need for acceptance, or protecting ourselves through rebellion and control. All of which are detrimental to a call to sonship and leadership. We should take responsibility for and repent from giving place to rejection and shame, renew our mind by the Word of God, receive the Father's love daily, and release forgiveness to any that have legitimately wounded or rejected us to bring closure to the past.

The circumstances that marked us with our deepest rejection and the places we find most difficult to push through often hide significant arenas of influence in our lives. The enemy works to not only silence our contribution to God's Kingdom but also to repel us from our greatest places of authority.[2]

Pride and Ambition

Pride presumes a position of superiority and prominence, and ambition seeks to drive us into a place of perceived success while side stepping the principles and ways of God. Musicians are susceptible to both because of the nature of entertainment and performance. We are trained all of our lives to compare, compete, and be successful. Absalom is a key character to study here because a root of ambition caused him to attempt to displace his own father, David (see 2 Sam. 15). He was ultimately unsuccessful, although for a season it seemed as though his personal ambition would propel him into a place of prominence. One of the most dangerous places to be is prospering outside of God's principles through pride and ambition. It is quite simple, and Proverbs 16:18 puts it clearly—if you insist on choosing pride, then you can expect to fall.

The draw toward pride is simply a strategy to cut off the flow of God's operational power into our lives because it is clear that He opposes the proud, but extends grace to those who walk in humility. (See Prov. 3:34; James 4:6.) We also need to understand that humility cannot be measured outwardly by man's standard but only Heaven's. A religious spirit will work with the spirit of pride to lock us into deception, self-righteousness, and powerlessness.

The Spirit of Heaviness

The spirit of heaviness manifests particularly against Praise and Worship to counteract the joy, life, and vitality being released from Heaven. It brings an opposite assignment against what is inherently ours as sons and daughters. Heaviness seeks to place a lid and limit upon the journey Godward and into the reality of being seated with Him and living in Heaven's atmosphere. It also seeks to silence proclamation and declaration by placing a blanket of lethargy. We must resist heaviness in all of its various forms including depression, sadness, lethargy, passivity, and hopelessness.

We must recognize when heaviness comes to restrict and constrict us and break its power from our lives. Consistently living in a realm of praise and being saturated with all that is present in Heaven causes heaviness to have no hold on our lives.

The Anti-Christ Spirit

The spirit of anti-Christ as its name suggests sets itself up against Christ and seeks to displace Him in the lives and minds of man. As we move into regions where this spirit is manifesting through false religion or a specific culture, we must know that it is designed to prevent the release of true praise and worship, or at least to pervert its focus. This spirit is literally *anti-Christ*. It is against His Kingdom, His anointing, His dominion and purpose. Apostolic worship breaks through the power of this spirit because of the authority it carries to legislate Christ's rule. We need to guard against all that comes to dethrone Christ as the King of nations in our lives, corporate worship, and every sphere of society.

Jezebel

In Revelation 2:20 the Jezebel Spirit is revealed as operating in the Church at Thyatira, but is first mentioned in First Kings 16:29-34 as the wife of King Ahab, a rebellious and manipulative woman who by the spirit operating through her caused almost the whole nation of Israel to bow to the false god Baal (see Rev. 2:20; 1 Kings 18:22). They abandoned the Covenant, destroyed the altars of the Lord and murdered the prophets of God. The word Jezebel means *without cohabitation,* and this spirit's primary purpose is to control and dominate. This will manifest in various ways. This spirit was the motivation behind the beheading of John the Baptist, Samson losing his vision, and the fall of the Church in Thyatira (see Rev. 2:20).

This spirit often uses various forms of perversity to capture individuals and families or even churches. We must understand though, that immorality is simply a means of gaining *control and inflicting powerlessness*. For example, an enticement to pornography, although a symptom of a deeper brokenness, can go ahead of a move of God attempting to kill God's purposes, take the ability to fight and silencing the war cry of individuals or the Church. Jezebel killed the true prophets of God and today this spirit still seeks to silence the prophetic because of its hatred of purity and holiness. This demonic entity hates repentance as this truly requires people to rely upon the grace, mercy and goodness of God as their source of righteousness. Not satisfied with removing the prophets, Jezebel also surrounded herself with eunuchs. This speaks of men that had been castrated— men who were emasculated and powerless to take their place.

Much of the entertainment industry is susceptible, and musicians can *operate* under the influence of a Jezebel spirit because of the perceived necessity to captivate, entice and control through performance and music. This spirit also comes against lead worshipers and musicians, especially those with a prophetic call. In relating to many Soundforgers, it is clear that the enemy often attempts to defile them at an early age through lust, pornography, or even sexual abuse. It is interesting that the steps to sexual defilement outlined in Romans chapter 1 hinges upon the central theme of worship. It is clear that those who have refused to worship the living God and instead worship *created things* are given over to unnatural perversion. This is why many of those called to be a hinge-place between Heaven and earth in worship—those who are to live in and lead others into the presence of God—are so violently attacked in this area.

Jezebel and other similar spirits will seek to entice us from operating in our true identity. As sons and daughters of a higher Kingdom, we must guard our eye gate, thought life, and heart motives and engage in adequate depth of accountability with others. As mentioned, strategic circumstances can be set up by the enemy to cause us to fall in weak areas. A spirit of perversion or *calling spirit* can operate through individuals and attack others that tolerate Jezebel in their thought life or secret place of their hearts. We can sometimes find ourselves strangely attracted to someone for no other reason than a spirit is operating to seduce us. If we are highly prophetic we can also experience a sense of *defilement* through discerning sexual sin in others or geographic places. The gift of discernment can work against us if we wrongly believe sudden or unnatural thoughts or feelings belong to us—when in fact we are perceiving the dominant *atmosphere* surrounding someone else's life.[3]

In Second Kings 9:31 we see Jehu rising as a type and shadow of those that will war against this spirit (see 2 Kings 9:31). He demands that Jezebel's own eunuchs throw her down from a high tower and then tramples her underfoot. We should exercise zero toleration for this demonic spirit while offering incredible mercy to those captivated and oppressed by it. It is important to highlight that this spirit will use men or women as a vehicle to influence and control. Many strong, godly women have been wounded by being labeled as a Jezebel when they are simply moving in the call of God where men may have not taken their place.[4]

A snapshot of these specific spirits highlights the need for increased awareness and wisdom in walking out our lives practically. Spirits can often work together in pairs or groups to strengthen position or develop a stronghold or entrenched pattern of behavior. They also attempt to work alongside any areas of unforgiveness, wounding or generational iniquity that may be present in our lives. Soundforgers must be sure to receive personal ministry in any areas to ensure that there is no potential place for the enemy's advantage. It is not necessary for us to live with hidden issues, brokenness, or sin. The ultimate price has been paid for our freedom!

ENDNOTES

1. Contains concepts from *Overcoming the Religious Spirit* by Rick Joyner (Morning Star Publications), and teaching by Julie Anderson,

Prayer for the Nations, (London).

2.   Contains concepts from *Explaining Rejection* by Steve Hebden (Sovereign World Ltd., 1992).

3.   Concept taken from Chapter Two, *Why Good People Mess Up*, John Loren Sandford, (Lake Mary, FL: Charisma House, 2007), 35-53.

4.   Contains concepts from various teachings by Barbara J. Yoder and Francis Frangipane on the spirit of Jezebel.

Chapter 11

Fathering the Soundforgers

The fathering and mentoring of emerging Soundforgers is a critical function in the activation and release of healthy lead-worshipers in the coming season.[1] It has been my experience that many emerging leaders wrongly identify the pathway to their future in separating themselves from the previous generation, and operate in rejecting all that has gone before them. Many wrongly believe that the only successful way to emerge is through consistent independence, self-sufficiency, and self-preservation. This has often been the strategy to cripple and deter many incredible leaders from moving into their God-given destiny, and one of many reasons why revival pockets that impacted society have usually never moved beyond one generation.[2] Equally, many have been subject to abusive spiritual parents who have misused the giftings and callings of those they have been given to nurture. However, we are in a transition in our understanding of cross-generational transfer.

There was no one as radical as Jesus who did only what he saw His Father doing. King David also understood not only the honoring of his spiritual and natural fathers but clearly walked out the long and extended promotion place with an unwillingness to dismiss God's previous General. The fact that David knew his call and anointing for kingship all along makes this even more incredible to me—and opens a doorway of understanding for us that God often calls the unqualified, who carry hidden seeds of greatness, and then qualifies them in a way that causes this very same seed to germinate.

Throughout this whole process, the richness of our hearts' soil is determined by our choice to live aligned with Heaven and our willingness to walk out the valleys as well as the mountains. As emerging Soundforgers, we need to live with an extended zeal for our destinies and the course of history in our generation while esteeming the place of security in our identity simply as sons and daughters of God. Making the decision to live in a way that causes neither the criticism nor the praise of man to move us is important. By doing this, we will be empowered to fully embrace and pass the tests of seasons where the true identities of Saul and David are both hidden, and where the insignificant are revealed as giant slayers. In my vision described in the opening chapter, the emerging Soundforgers were presented with tests that they had choices to embrace. The greatest tests from God are the ones that you do not even know you are taking. I have personally failed many and been offered the opportunity to take them over again, without being dismissed by God or losing my place in the journey!

We can be quick to qualify or disqualify radical emerging leaders by mistakes, the color of their hair, or other signs of outward statement rather than the inward furnishing of the imprint of God that is rising. Some of the most radical people I know are the sons and daughters of martyrs from the Middle East who are now in training for the call of God on their own lives. Many of these leaders operate unseen, yet have passed the test of overcoming hatred for those who killed their family members and attempted to cut short their call and birthright. They have been marked and branded inwardly through passing many fire-filled challenges. I believe that some of them will do exactly what they hear their Heavenly Father saying and doing and will usher in spiritual reformation and societal transformation in the very countries where the blood of their families was spilled for the cause of Christ.

Multi-generational operation is an entirely biblical concept, and embracing this paradigm from whichever side of the age spectrum we are on is not an option but a necessity if we are to move into fulfilling all that God has for us. Whether emerging leaders have been sidelined, shut down, or misunderstood, or established leaders dishonored, worshiped or forced to abdicate, it is clear that the Father still works through *Sonship* as He has done since the days of Adam, throughout Jesus' ministry and in the early Church.

In the first direct reference to music in Genesis 4:21, *Jubal* is called the *father* of all who play the harp and flute (see Gen. 4:21). It was exciting to discover this Scripture because as a *first mention* passage it holds keys of understanding that unlock principles of God. Scripture also says that around this time men also began to proclaim and call on the name of the Lord (see Gen. 4:26). It is interesting that the first musician is called a "Father of all that came after" and was familiar with and surrounded daily by brothers who operated in specific spheres—a *shepherd* who watched and guarded, and a *metal forger* who would have shaped tools for agricultural, construction and warfare purposes. For me, these three partner together in the form of a modern-day lead worshiper: a shepherding musician that proclaims and calls on the name of the Lord, forging sound that tends the ground of men's hearts, builds and sets in place after God's design and goes to war.

The Spirit of God spoke clearly to me that there was a new generation of apostolic and prophetic spiritual fathers and mothers in the arena of worship who were looking for sons and daughters to impart to in this season—that many Elishas had been prepared and were currently positioned intensely plowing *hardened* ground with 12 yolks of oxen (1 Kings 19:19b). As 12 is biblically the number of government and order, this symbolizes among other things, the apprentice place of learning to cooperate and plow with aspects of governmental function and anointing. These emerging ones are on the edge of being called alongside Elijahs in a new dimension. A dream I had a number of years ago highlighted the issue of spiritual fathering for musicians. In this night vision, Keith Green was searching for me as I worshiped, and the desire I had for him to simply release a father's blessing over me grew as I searched for him. The dream ended as we found each other and he imparted God's heart to me in prayer.

THE ELISHA GENERATION

Fathering is a key that enables one generation to go further than its predecessor. James W. Goll in his article, "The Elisha Generation" says:

A generation that is placed upon the shoulders of the fathers and mothers who have gone before them and a generation of believing believers who walk in security of identity of the Fatherhood of God will be the Greater Works Generation that Jesus declared was coming. John 14:12 declares, *"And greater works then these shall you do; because I go to the Father."* **It is time for authentic fathers and mothers in the Word and Spirit to arise and invest their lives into the next generation.** They are those who are genuine veterans of the ways of God and pioneers who have blazed a trail for others. It is time for the Greater Works Generation to arise—who know the Father, who magnify the Son and who live in the Spirit.[3]

Elisha cried out for the double portion, not just for himself, but for his entire generation. He knew that in order to impact, it would take more of God's grace and power than had rested on the previous generation.

James Goll illustrates that we can learn much from Elisha's response:

- **He *served* in another's sphere.**
- **He *passed the tests presented* and picked up his own cross.**
- **He *saw* in the Spirit.**
- **He *lifted a cry*.**
- **He understood *honor*.**

- **He had a revelation of *fatherhood*.**
- **He *received his inheritance* and acted it out!**

Receiving, protecting, equipping, positioning and releasing emerging Soundforgers will be crucial elements in these days, if we are to see them properly aligned within fullness of their giftings and purpose. Correct alignment with leadership is an incredibly awesome Kingdom principal that we are understanding more and more, but still musicians are susceptible to moving out in independence because of a variety of factors that we will discuss later in this chapter. My senior leader Terry Moore explains that there are three levels of *leadership*—covering, mentoring, and fathering. The familiar verse "you have many instructors but not many fathers" speaks to this (see 1 Cor. 4:15). Leadership in its most basic form provides *covering,* the next level of operation is *mentoring,* but the desired level in this generation is *fathering*. The cost is too high for us to remain as instructors only.

I am grateful for incredible biological parents who nurtured, encouraged and released me into destiny throughout my life. In addition to this, at different times in my development personally and in ministry, the Holy Spirit has led me to be planted alongside specific spiritual leaders who have fathered me in significant ways. So far there have been five significant spiritual parents in my life who have nurtured and released me in crucial seasons—all of them have brought an element of insight and growth that I would not want to be without. Looking back, it is remarkable to see how each relationship sharpened, protected, and equipped me in different aspects of Kingdom life. Foundational discipleship, areas of inner healing and deliverance, in-depth principles of the Word, prophetic ministry and anointing, physical healing, mentoring in being a husband and father, finances, ministry protocol, correction, international vision, and missions, were all added to my life through God's chosen leadership. Obviously, a relationship with the Holy Spirit was my primary source of life and revelation, but earthly community was, and still is, invaluable and irreplaceable in my Kingdom development as a leader. Fathering provides relational mentoring for us that increases security, unlocks destiny and releases maturity. Imparting Heaven's blueprint with a father's heart moves us forward in supernatural ways. This is what I have experienced through various spiritual fathers and leaders. We have laughed together, gone to war together, cried, prayed, worked through conflict, counseled, loved, sacrificed, and honored each other.

I want to be careful here not to relay a picture of perfection because *real* Kingdom relationships have *real* challenges. In fact, we can carry past wounds from spiritual leadership, which hinder us from fully aligning ourselves with and honoring our current authority. It is crucial that we get healed from pain, released from negative patterns of relating to leadership, and restored into meaningful relationship with those who God has set us with. We may need to revisit former leaders and ask for forgiveness or explain how we were hurt. Disregarding past wounds will ultimately hinder us from moving into our destiny. We must be awakened to remove every hindrance to our future and every wall that prevents us from healthily relating to leaders. In the current season, more than ever before, correct alignment is not something that is negotiable. He will always lead us to be aligned with His Kingdom principle of family by rooting us in the local church even if we are ultimately called to go to nations. We must locate our particular *tribe* and connect.

At a fundamental level, an apostle's or pastor's anointing and position to cover, mentor and father is not dependant on whether he or she understands, endorses, or releases us; and hopefully all of these will be in place. But it is simply the positional authority that they have been given and is part of the spiritual equipment that they carry. When we truly understand spiritual authority, no matter what stage of our assignment we are in, we will pursue it at every given opportunity. Once my wife and I received the revelation of the key of leadership, we sought to pursue transition from one set of authority to another in a healthy way. Even with a right heart motive and applying Kingdom principles, there have been challenges. Sometimes, our lack of communication or own immaturity or inability to perceive the timing of God caused a problem in the place of transition. At times our leader's reluctance to let us go caused us to entertain fear that we would be controlled and blocked from moving forward in God. However, the depth of relationship and love always compelled us and our leaders to walk out the transition correctly. Each of our senior leaders has enabled us to move forward by sending and releasing us into the next phase of God for our lives. I can honestly say that today we are not dislocated from any of our previous leadership relationships. We are not in regular contact with some, but our friendships are not fractured or hiding festering wounds and areas of significant disagreement.

Some of the blessings of being sent include: a secure and clean transition into the new place of assignment without transporting spiritual baggage, relational support-bridges remaining while new ones are built, and evidence of the favor of God because of the endorsement of our previous leadership. Relational trust is also protected in the old and affirmed in the new spiritual family. Healthy transition is also modeled within the previous Body as faithful people are released over your area of ministry. There are many reasons why shifting location within Kingdom principles is a good idea. The bottom line is—it is a God idea.

Much of what David set in place in Tabernacle Worship was relational in that people were set in place as families and under the supervision of fathers. David raised up three leaders, who themselves raised up hundreds. I know that effective lead worshipers such as Martin Smith, Matt Redman, Chris Tomlin, Charlie Hall, Misty Edwards, Jason Upton, David Crowder, have spiritual communities, mentors or fathers who consistently restore their cutting edge. In the Book of Samuel, the axe head that the sons of the prophets were using to cut down trees for the *next place of habitation* was accidentally lost in the river, but was supernaturally restored by Elisha—the spiritual father in this situation (see 2 Kings 6:1-7). When the place is too small for a generation, when vision in the nation is diminished, when hope for our future is seemingly small and we temporarily lose our ability to penetrate into building for the next season, spiritual fathers meet us there and engage in restoring our cutting edge, enabling us to move out of stagnation and we begin to build a new, enlarged place according to the Father's design.

EMERGING SOUNDFORGERS

At a think-tank gathering focused upon receiving a heart and strategy for the emerging generation, led by Doug Stringer, founder of Somebody Cares, the Lord revealed several keys to us that are crucial in seeing emerging Soundforgers surface. They are going to require:

- *Permission and endorsement* to define their own sound and voice.

- Assistance in *navigating* between anti-traditionalism and cross-generational transfer.

- Release to operate with *increased relevance* to their own generation.

- Awareness of the necessity to *inherit the creativity* they are called to possess and encouragement to walk in that creativity—seeing the future in what is coming, not necessarily modeling the now.

- A one-on-one *support system* that will operate relationally, built through serving and never prostituting.

- *Nurturing* through grassroots, organic, and authentic models.

- *Relevant venues and platforms* being made available for music that operates outside traditional church models—releasing pre-conversion discipleship.

- **Networks** that support those who carry these core values. At Soundforgers, we are developing networks that will equip and connect emerging musicians and worshipers in regions throughout the world.[4]

These practical keys are a starting place in relating correctly and can be built upon as transition moves into actuality. If we believe that God is restoring the Tabernacle of David and releasing the key of David in the midst of our cities and nations, the prophetic and apostolic musicians are today a key element in this fullness as they were in ancient Israel. As in the days of Nehemiah's temple restoration, modern day Levites have often been exiled and have gathered in dwelling places they have *built for themselves*. It is time for them to be sought out, fathered and restored to their position (see Neh.12:27-28).

THE SPIRIT OF FATHERING AND THE RESPONSE OF SONS AND DAUGHTERS

As important as fathering is, the necessity to **receive** it as a son or daughter is proportionately crucial. We can unknowingly operate out of an **orphan spirit** that prevents us from being able to receive meaningful love and live in healthy relationships. Foremost is the need to experience and receive the love of *the* Father. Jesus received this when He was baptized and the Holy Spirit descended on Him. The Father's heart was undeniable—"You are my Son, whom I love; with you I am well pleased" (Luke 3: 22). This foundation of the love of the Father was a major key in the warfare He encountered as the enemy later confronted Him in the wilderness. Satan's question "If you are the Son of God, tell these stones to become bread" (Matt. 4:3) is not so much questioning Jesus' **ability** to do the miracle, but challenging his **identity** as the Son of God. The "Did God really say?" factor has been the enemy's strategy from the beginning in the Garden (see Gen. 3:1).

But Jesus answers according to the Word of the Father:

It is written: Man does not live on bread alone, but on every word that comes from the mouth of God (Matthew 4:4).

He clearly makes a declaration that He does not live by the affirmation of performing miracles—but on the love of His Father who had previously spoken! This is an incredible foundation for us as we live saturated and affirmed in the love of God and walk out our call and destiny from that place.[5]

RECEIVING SOUNDFORGERS

The dictionary definition of *receiving* unpacks some great concepts for us. It means, "to take or acquire; to hear or see; to meet with and experience; to bear the weight or force of; to support; to take in, hold, or contain; to greet or welcome; to perceive or acquire mentally; to listen to and acknowledge formally and authoritatively."

Whether sons and daughters are undeveloped or relatively mature, there is a powerful transaction that takes place in their spirits when they are actively received and activated by fathers or mentors.

Speaking validity to what is emerging is vital in providing a platform of faith for sons and daughters to continue to step out into unknown territory. Apostolic and prophetic Soundforgers require permission and endorsement to define their own sound and voice, in actuality, to be an expression of the Father's sound and voice in the earth.

In my own personal life, although gifted outwardly, I was equally crippled inwardly through rejection. The experiences of life without the reality of God, along with the words, actions, and responses of people, had done damage to me in the soul realm that Jesus literally reached into and rearranged. Some of my spiritual fathers and mentors have no idea how God used them to change my life in this area alone. There is a Mephibosheth generation (see 2 Sam. 9:1-3) that is literally being restored from a disinherited, crippled state by the acceptance and restoration spearheaded by kingly fathers.

So Mephibosheth ate at David's table like one of the king's sons (2 Samuel 9:11).

In the connecting of the generations I have heard both sides of the argument—that sons should be the ones to pursue fathers and that fathers should pursue sons. It can work either way as long as we ultimately find ourselves in relationship, and sons find themselves received by fathers (see Mal. 4:5-6). I personally relate to both needing influential leaders in my life and the challenge of pursing those individuals as mentors. For many emerging leaders this is often intimidating but ultimately demands that they push through feelings of inadequacy and false humility—which is the very thing God is requiring of them. However, these are also the very arrows of dysfunction that can be removed by spiritual fathers who will pursue them. As far as I can see from my own research, mentoring relationships in the Word of God are weighted on the side of mentors pursuing disciples. Elijah hearing from God to walk with Elisha, Samuel calling David out of obscurity, Paul fathering Timothy, and Jesus pursuing all of His disciples are some clear examples.

Regardless, Soundforgers need to be open to receive fathers and fathers to receive Sons. The meeting place of the zeal of the young and the wisdom of the old is going to position us for the favor and power to impact our generation together. The damage of neglect and rejection is being displaced in those that are emerging. Through pioneers carrying the Father's heart, the ceiling of the past season is becoming the ground floor for the next generation.

PROTECTING SOUNDFORGERS

To *protect* means "to keep something from being damaged, attacked, stolen or injured; to intentionally guard and defend."

I have learned through some difficult experiences that God places leaders in our lives not to restrict and limit us but to watch over, and to a certain extent, be a protection for us. Through relational-based support systems, leaders can build sons without ever restricting or selfishly using their gifting or abilities. A paradigm of protecting in order to secure full future emergence is key for fathering Soundforgers.

Early on as a worship leader, people began to invite me to various places to minister—recognizing gifting and not always questioning maturity! I remember one experience that defined the need for an adjustment. My concept of adequate covering and fathering dramatically changed. I took a trip to the North of England to what I understood to be a young church plant, and after speaking with the pastor beforehand felt that we were carrying a similar heart for the things of God and the direction that He was moving. After arriving, the pastor explained that he wanted to release the leadership of the entire meeting over to me. This had not happened before to this extent, and I was excited at the possibility of having so much freedom to stretch out. The Lord had already downloaded pages of notes relating to the church that I felt could be prophesied and communicated. It was looking like a God moment. I had been given some revelation for the corporate direction of the church, and much of what God had revealed leaned into a pastoral anointing in personal ministry, healing, and God's desire for restoration out of woundedness. I was quickly going to find out why!

I forgot to mention that I had not asked or told Sam Yeghnazar, my senior leader at the time, about the assignment. The pastor of the church we were visiting had also chosen not to tell me that the church he was leading existed as a result of a split that had just happened a few weeks earlier and that this group had left in rebellion due to some painful disagreements. To say that I felt oppressed the morning I was supposed to lead is an understatement. No matter how I prayed or worshiped, I began to feel increasingly fearful, vulnerable, and spiritually exposed. I have to say that the pastor had inherited a difficult situation and was not personally responsible for the split and clearly had a heart for the people, attempting to make the best from a bad situation. He did, however, lack discernment in releasing a place of leadership to me that I had anointing but not authority to walk in.

Anointing does not necessarily translate into authority. We may have been furnished with the Holy Spirit for a key purpose in a setting but may not hold *the* key of leadership or authority in the situation. We can sometimes confuse anointing in the *moment* with having automatic authority to cover, lead and direct. This is not the case.

As I continued to prepare, I felt increasingly uneasy and less peace filled but stepped out in releasing all that the Holy Spirit had revealed to me about the church. Because of God's incredible faithfulness, the time was amazingly fruitful, considering the circumstances—and afterward, people reported different degrees of emotional healing and forgiveness. In retrospect I was not carrying enough authority—spiritually or geographically—to handle the brokenness and the warfare surrounding that particular situation. The pastor had attempted to fix a *governmental* problem with an *anointing* answer. As I traveled home and asked the Lord about the situation, He talked firmly to me about my independence, telling me to meet with my pastor later and repent for my pride and lack of seeking counsel. I am glad to say that my pastor listened knowingly, ministered to me and affirmed his love for me. This is not to say that I have never encountered intense spiritual intimidation when properly aligned or sent. But it is clear that continuing in an independent spirit would have been detrimental to the plan of God for my life. Independence and rebellion are linked in their source but differ in their outworking. Independence is a propensity toward operating alone and carving for ourselves special permission to function without inter-dependence and accountability. Rebellion is the direct disrespect and overt rejection of authority—often deliberately going against God-given boundaries. I operated in an independent spirit because I wrongly presumed through pride that I had spiritual weight to handle the situation alone. If I had been specifically told not to minister in that setting by God or my pastor—and still insisted on going—then I would have stepped into rebellion also. The problem in this ministry situation was not in *what* I did, but *how* I walked it out. A greater degree of *sent-ness* would have provided protection for me from the absence of true spiritual order and government.

There are legitimate and illegitimate processes of positioning and promotion. Which one we choose ultimately starts in the secret places of our hearts. Those closest to us who have *permission* as well as *position* over us are best qualified to see our blind spots. The enemy uses illegitimate avenues of promotion and will attempt to draw us into using those methods as a means to advance ourselves in God's Kingdom ahead of time. As we already touched upon earlier, we can obviously never stand in true authority that has not been delegated or released to us. As in any arena of ministry, our healing must be paramount because rejection, shame, and ambition will drive us to make decisions that are detrimental. I believe that a root of pride and immaturity can cause us to move out in independence and not recognize God's order in promoting us legitimately. We can become so enamoured with taking on a battle alone and emerging with the trophies that can seemingly cause us to look so good that we sometimes disregard simple biblical boundaries. Pride is a dangerous place, and I am so grateful for the personal wake-up call that now shapes ministry decisions and direction. I usually run all ministry invitations through my Senior Pastor and personal intercessors. Together we hear God and attempt to correctly understand the ministry situation, the connected relationships, timing, possible weak places in the wall, and possible travel companions before moving forward. As ever, it is a challenge for a bold David generation to move in God's assignments correctly aligned with life-giving relationships without having to go in Saul's armor! God can be pouring music through us that has the potential to change nations but this does not automatically mean that our full potential will be realized, especially if we refuse to walk within Kingdom principles.

There are so many facets to protecting emerging Soundforgers. Holistically, these include guarding against pride, wrong alliances, inappropriate relationships, bad financial decisions, and living with hidden sin issues. I am not condoning a situation where every decision in life is screened by a spiritual father or mother, but key life decisions and potentially destructive patterns can be successfully navigated through trust and connectedness.

EQUIPPING SOUNDFORGERS

To equip indicates a furnishing for success and help in growth and development— implying cultivation, education and training.

Equipping works together with fathering to produce supernatural results in a person's life. Practical equipping in arenas of teamwork, leadership skills, spiritual government, corporate dynamics, family,

healthy relationships, finances, and time management strengthen
the success base underneath emerging musicians and cause support
walls to be in place that prevent derailing. So many incredibly
anointed lead worshipers cut short or damage what God has released
to them because of practical character issues that have never been
resolved. Equipping in how to walk in integrity and purity is also
foundational. In Christ we are clearly no longer sinners but seated in
heavenly places and cannot work our way to righteousness before
God. However, there are clear principles of leadership running
throughout the Word of God that speak to character and purity
issues. The Lord does release assignments to weak, unconfident people but it is not His plan to prematurely commission unhealed, unpre-
pared vessels that will shipwreck and cause damage to the Bride and
the Kingdom. Humility and a heart after purity—not perfection—
position us for success in knowing that success depends upon Him
but that we have enormous responsibility to adequately align character with destiny.

On another practical level, financial provision and equipping for
those emerging musicians is an important issue. It has been the
greatest area of battle in my life—one where breakthrough has come,
and where I am crying *restore* in the realm of the spirit for every called
Soundforger positioned in the nations.

> *I also learned that the portions assigned to the Levites had
> not been given to them, and that all the Levites and singers
> responsible for the service had gone back to their own fields*
> (Nehemiah 13:10).

This is an interesting statement at the end of a book that deals primarily with restoration. The Levites returned to their fields and built towns for themselves because adequate provision was not made for them. The word "provision"—means exactly that: *pro-vision*—that which facilitates the vision. There has been a significant lack of vision in the creative arena of the Church, and musicians have historically perished. It is crucial to provide the adequate resources to build a platform for success underneath emerging Soundforgers. Adequate financial provision should be in place to enable the gift to function unhindered. For the most part, there has been a blind spot in the Body of Christ in regard to providing for His psalmists and often, usually unintentionally, their gifting has been misused and abused. Inadequate funds have been allocated for the ministry of the psalmist, forcing them to work in part time relatively low-paid employment that does not require 100 percent of their time and energy so that very little creativity can flow. Or on the contrary, salaries are provided but with a high level of control and administrative expectation upon the gifting that quenches creativity and disables the fullness emerging. Breakthrough is coming as significant numbers of ministries and churches recognize the particular environment in which creativity flourishes. If we desire the best out of these musicians for the Kingdom, it is crucial that the area of provision or lack of it does not become a distraction or avenue to divert destiny.

Much in the area of equipping exists to develop and encourage existing deposits of God in raising Soundforgers. We must be committed to releasing radical and unstoppable sons and daughters for war who will be stabilized in every area so that they will not be shipwrecked.

Correct equipping allows a unique creative fingerprint to develop, a unique voice to be clarified, an assignment to be perceived. For example, those with strong prophetic gifts may not reach full development if boxed into a pastoral paradigm. However, elements of pastoral understanding will add great strength to strong prophetic gifting. A gift of mercy may be evident and need extensive nurturing in someone's life because of the extent of governmental authority God is calling them into. Great authority requires an equally great deposit of mercy and kindness, which balances the level of Kingdom demonstration and power God is intending. Proper equipping is non-negotiable.

POSITIONING SOUNDFORGERS

To position something means to engage in the act or process of aligning it in the right or appropriate place. *Position* can describe a strategic area occupied by members of a force; the arrangement of separate parts of a whole; an advantageous place or location; or a situation as it relates to the surrounding circumstances.

Correct positioning begins with a correct analysis of where we are currently and continued response in each season that the Lord has us in. Fathers who know God (see 1 John 2:13) can help musicians to understand what each particular season requires of them and how to position correctly for the next. The emerging leaders think tank I mentioned earlier identified the necessity for Soundforgers to inherit the creativity they are called to possess, seeing the future in what is coming, not necessarily modeling the "now." It will require specific alignment and positioning to walk out this fresh paradigm.

There are many ways to position ourselves correctly to inherit the future. Some possibilities are to:

- Correctly interpret where we are within the plan of God for our lives.

- Identify the next steps to move forward into what God has revealed.

- Identify any blockages to taking the appropriate steps.

- Identify where we are off track and align in the right direction in each area of our lives.

- Position ourselves strategically for a launch into the new.

- Embrace the rearrangement and positioning of rela- tionships, resources, geography, finances, etc.

It takes specific reality checks and definite adjustments to begin to be positioned correctly.

Praying into our future is another tool we have been given to secure accurate positioning. We are to contend with roadblocks, cry out to Heaven and pray into the future before we even get there!

Prayer initiatives help us be sensitized ahead of time as to what our challenges will be and also what Heaven's answers are. Prayer also enables us to be personally sensitized to correctly interpret where we are on God's timeline.

In terms of personal positioning, there have been many different seasons that I have navigated through. Record and publishing contracts, cross-cultural missions, relocating to another nation, leading worship and training musicians in various corporate settings from the local church to national gatherings, and working between churches, ministries, and the marketplace. We are aware of several big picture aspects to the call on our family that help us stay on target. One of these is the mandate I received to help equip the emerging generation. This came through a series of impressions from the Lord, prophetic visions, prophetic words and counsel with established leaders. This was not something that I presumed quickly and it has taken me several years of adjustment to begin to see the outworking of the vision. When I arrived in the United States as a worship pastor, I had previously been engaged under another ministry in gathering the Body of Christ from across the nation in England for a stadium event. At the end of this pivotal time, the Lord's call to the United States came particularly strong and clear, and our spiritual leadership at the time released us. After arriving in the States, I felt impressed to work at a grassroots level––feeling led to input and pour into only a couple of young musicians as well as my worship team. This was different to the previous assignment and the Lord required me to simply operate on a local level. This became one of the ways that He released legitimate authority to us in a new geographic region. This has been a pattern for us as we moved from one assignment to another. The stewardship of worship teams for the stadium event came after five years of praying and worshiping in a basement house of prayer in London. The Lord sometimes wants to see if we can be trusted with a few before opening the doors to more. This book is the fruit of many different seasons of responding and journeying and being correctly positioned to equip. It is one of the resources that will help fulfill the vision of raising and releasing Soundforgers and the new sound Heaven is bringing.

RELEASING SOUNDFORGERS

To *release* means "to set free from confinement, restraint, or bondage; to free from something that binds, fastens, or holds back; to dismiss from one position to another; to relinquish (a right or claim); a deliverance from confinement or restraint; an authoritative discharge, as from an obligation or from prison; an unfastening or letting go of something caught or held fast."

The fathering and equipping places as we have already mentioned are irreplaceable. But emerging leaders do not find their ultimate fulfillment until they are actually *released* into their destiny within the Kingdom.

> Now Ben-Hadad King of Aram mustered his entire army. He sent messengers into the city to Ahab King of Israel, saying "This is what Ben-Hadad says: Your silver and gold are mine, and the best of your wives and children are mine." The king

of Israel answered, "Just as you say, my lord the king. I and all I have are yours (1 Kings 20:1-4).

In this passage, the authority in the land is in agreement with the plan of the enemy to plunder and steal, and is even willing to give up its inheritance—delivering the best of the wives and children into the possession of the enemies of God. Fortunately, the Word of the Lord comes through a prophet:

Meanwhile a prophet came to Ahab King of Israel and announced, "This is what the Lord says: 'Do you see this vast army? I will give it into your hand today, and then you will know that I am the Lord.'"
"But who will do this?" asked Ahab.
The prophet replied, "This is what the Lord says: 'the young officers of the provincial commanders will do it.'"
"And who will start the battle?" he asked.
The prophet answered, "You will" (1 Kings 20:13-14).

It is great to hear God's perspective when leadership has given into fear!

In this passage, young warriors are released into war by God and the "fathers" and breakthrough comes. It takes an experienced generation, willing to release at the God moment those who have been prepared and positioned--willing to see them surpass and overtake all that they may have accomplished in an entire lifetime. This is the privilege of generational transference. There is a generation being propelled into their destiny who will surpass us in zeal and confidence in God if the *generations* will now prepare and function as they are intended to. Let us receive, protect, equip, position and release a generation of Heaven-hearers to see the necessary breakthrough in our generation.

> *Your troops will be willing on your day of battle. Arrayed in holy majesty, from the womb of the dawn you will receive the dew of your youth* (Psalm 110:3).

ENDNOTES

1.   The term "fathering" is used throughout this chapter but is not meant to be gender exclusive in terms of its function. Women can and do carry the spirit of parenting, and mentoring is an interchangeable term in this chapter. "Fathering" served our purpose better for this book.

2.   Bill Johnson, Bethel Church, Redding, CA.

3.   James W. Goll, *The Elisha Generation* article, Encounters Network, February 25, 2005; http://www.encountersnetwork.com/email_blasts/feb_2005_en.html.

4.   www.soundforgers.org.

5.   Concepts taken from *Free Indeed* training manual, Terry Moore, (Dallas, TX: Sojourn Church, 2007), 16.

C h a p t e r   1 2

Implementation

It is time for implementation. An ancient tribe carrying a new sound is being named and activated by Heaven. They are by nature Heaven-hearers, called to receive and release the sounds and songs of Heaven into the earth.

This new sound is a Kingdom sound. It is a corporate sound. It is the sound of sons set free, bodies healed, it is a sound of justice and mercy, of love and war. It is a sound that *engages* the church as a cap-tivated Bride and *activates* Her as the apostolic church. It is a sound that contributes to the increase of His government and peace (see Isa. 9:7). It is the sound of apostolic declaration that legislates the release of Heaven on earth. It is a sound that carries the governmental key of David. It is a sound that unlocks the gates to our cities and regions by decrees and declarations from the mouth of the Bride. Do you hear it? Do you carry it? Destiny is waiting.

Soundforgers, it is time for you to take the key of no reputation and watch it become a Key of Government in your hand. Stand between Heaven and earth and engage the strategic places of tran-sition. Heaven's atmosphere and Heaven's sound is here to legislate.

Let the Bridegroom play you, let Him speak through you. Let Him fill and enlarge your sound and your voice. This is bigger than you, greater than church, more than a conference. It is about the Kingdom of our God and the transformation of our cities and regions. There is a vast army of musicians emerging who carry the favor and anointing of God on their lives. They are quickly moving from priestly mediation to apostolic proclamation. They will not hold back the words of God in the days ahead. They will not hold back the fresh wind of Heaven being released. They will play their part in history in taking entire regions with the atmosphere of Heaven. The very regions of the earth where it seems that the light of God may go out, our God has marked for Himself. Many are awakening in prayer, declaration, and bold action. Teams of governmental Sound-forgers will go into the nations with apostles and prophets, and together they will see massive breakthrough in cities and regions. The Church will be revived and restored as the Lion roars again. Even areas of Europe that are dead and dry will be revitalized. The Middle East will know the Son and the demonstration of His Kingdom. The release of the sounds and songs of Heaven will echo in the nations! Sound what you hear Him sounding and declare what you hear Him declaring. See the atmosphere of Heaven displace defeat, apathy and division in the Church, and disease, death, and disillusionment in our cities!

Areas of society that have been hidden from the music of Heaven are getting ready to be invaded with a sound that brings awakening and life. Fresh initiatives in education, government, media, arts and entertainment are emerging; are breaking through and bringing the

Kingdom. This is not a season to hold back but to move forward in prophetic understanding and apostolic authority.

Our corporate sound will no longer be marked by sentiment, self-comfort or self-preservation because God is bringing swift realignment. As Soundforgers relinquish their sound and song, they are being entrusted with His. The Church is again hearing the sound of the Man of War as He moves over the Kingdoms of the earth. No longer just dwelling in intimacy but rising in God-given authority, the Church is finding her voice and her purpose. We will live and worship as those who are crowned—not just those who are saved and hiding. Kingdom worship is here to parallel the moves of God going to the streets, marketplace and nations. What it will sound like—He is shaping. Our part is to prepare for it, receive it and walk it out!

Walking It Out

- Live daily embracing **worship as a lifestyle.** Live as a son or daughter accessing limitless intimacy with God.
- Walk as a **Soundforger** in the earth. Seek God passionately. Receive the **sounds of Heaven** and become sensitized to forging and carrying the sound for the "now" in priestly, prophetic and apostolic worship.
- Seek to understand your spiritual **equipment and assignment.** Know what type of Soundforger you are and how you primarily move in God.
- Know your designated **sphere of authority** within your local church, city or region.

- With *practicing the presence of God* also **practice the release** of the priestly, prophetic and apostolic worship in personal times with God. Gain authority for the corporate out of the place of the personal. Be open to greater intimacy, revelation, and authority as you worship God in secret.

- Like Asaph, Heman, and Jeduthun be **faithful, enduring collectors of God's thoughts.** Grow in hearing sensitivity when spending time with God. Know when He is saying something that you need to harvest. Also listen intently to five-fold leaders and extract the language for today's and tomorrow's songs.

- **Contend for an anointing to match the truth of apostolic worship** so that it does not remain simply a biblical principle. Align with the Spirit of God to bring what Heaven is declaring into the earth realm.

- **Like Jacob,** wrestle with God in intimacy but also recognize the place of visitation and the open Heaven that is a present reality in your city and region.

- **Engage Kingdom mandates** in your life and expand the Kingdom wherever you are.

- In partnership with leadership, **move toward the inclusion** of priestly, prophetic, and apostolic songs in the corporate. Determine ahead of time the appropriateness of the moment and degree to which the specific group you are leading is ready to move into revelatory and declarative worship.

- Courageously move within your given **sphere of authority** and understand when and where you are released to move in higher levels through promotion or authority by association. Be faithful so that you can be personally released into greater measures of authority.

- Familiarize yourself with what God is doing in different spheres. **Every realm of society is waiting for transformation.** Marketplace, education, politics, government, family, church, and entertainment are all waiting to be influenced. Find your place and release the sound and song of Heaven.

- Operate as a grass-roots servant in the **local church**— working alongside leadership for the accomplishment of the vision of the house.

- **Guard the presence of God** in the arena you have been placed (1 Kings 11). Contend for seeds of revival to come to maturity.

- **Connect with strategic intercessors** in your local church and community. Consider partnering with a house of prayer—even for a short season.

- **Release decrees and declarations** over your personal life, family and church.

- Alongside established leadership and within your recognized sphere of authority**, release declarations in apostolic worship** for the good of the community— pre–Christian, education, local government, the needy and marginalized.

- Regularly be part of **city-wide,** cross-denominational, multigenerational gatherings. If invited to lead worship, out of relationship, humility and in full submission, dialogue with leadership as to your personal gift-mix in worship and the place and function of "strategic worship" in corporate gatherings.

- Lock in to the **prophetic words over the destiny** of your church, city, and lead worship accordingly. Recognize **kairos moments** in the life of your church, community, city, nation and lend yourself to what **apostles, prophets, and Church leaders** and churches are saying and initiating in your geographic area. Become increasingly aware of how you build alongside five-fold leadership.

- Walk in a **recover-all** mindset—complete restoration is possible according to 1 Samuel 30. Agree and partner with this Davidic anointing upon musicians to help individuals, congregations and cities recover all.

- Be a part of the **Soundforgers network** being established in major cities.

- As an **emerging leader,** walk in permission from God to be who you are. If you are leading emerging leaders, give adequate permission for them to be who they are.

- Be **fathered and intentionally father others** to see the receiving, protection, nurture, equipping, positioning and release of future generations.

- Seek to operate ***cross-generationally*** in as many spheres as possible—be open to receive wisdom as to how the strength of the generations marry and work together.

Open your mouths emerging generation. He is here and He is taking back the kingdoms of the Earth. We have lived as those whose time would come, and it is here. Your smooth stone is already in the sling. You did not go in Saul's armor, you prepared and consecrated, you defeated the lion and the bear, you were anointed in secret and now it is time. Open wide your mouth and release the sound that is both terrible and wonderful. Creation will know that the sons of God are being revealed. Become the sound and song of Heaven in the Earth!

I saw heaven standing open and there before me was a white horse, whose rider is Faithful and True. With justice he judges and makes war. His eyes are like blazing fire, and on his head are many crowns…. He is dressed in a robe dipped in blood, and his name is the Word of God…. Out of his mouth comes a sharp sword with which to strike down the nations…. On his robe and on his thigh he has this name written: King of kings and Lord of lords (Revelation 19: 11-13,15-16).

A p p e n d i x   A

PRIESTLY PSALMS

David

4:7-9	A full heart
5:3-9	Early morning
5:11-12	Refuge
8:1-9	Your Name and Glory
9:1-2	Sing and tell
13:5	Trust in Your unfailing love
16	My portion
18:1-7	My strength
19:14	The words of my mouth
23	Shepherd
27:7-9	Your face
28:6	Thankful
30:1, 11-12	Lifted me
31:19-23	Goodness
57:9-11	Exalted
59:16	Fortress
62:1-3	Rock and Salvation
63:1-9	Earnestly
65:4-13	Blessed
139	You know me

Sons of Korah

42:1	Thirsty
48:9	Unfailing love
84:1	Dwelling place

Asaph

73:23-27	Portion

Ethan

89:1	Faithfulness

Unknown

71:22	Shout for joy
92:1-9	Make music
115:1	Because of Your love
119:89-91	Faithfulness continues

PROPHETIC REVELATORY PSALMS

David

11:5	Revelation of the eyes of the Lord
12:5-7	I will now arise—His promise for the oppressed
14:2-3	Revelation that He is seeking
15	Revelatory instruction
19:1-7	Revelation of creation
22:1-25	Revelation of crucifixion
22:25-31	Revelation of the nations and future generations
27:1-4, 13	Revelation of His light and protection
29:3-11	The voice of the Lord
31:23	Be strong
32:8-10	I will instruct you and teach you

34:8	Taste and see
36	An oracle
37:1-9	Trust and wait
52:1-8	Word to unbelieving generation
53	God looks down to see if any seek Him
58:1	Question to earthly rulers
60:6-9	God speaks over His inheritance
62:5	Proclamation over our own lives
62:11	One thing God has spoken, two things I have heard
68:5	A Father to the fatherless
68:11	The Lord announced the word
69:35	Rebuilding the cities of Judah
108:7	God speaks over His inheritance
110:1	I make your enemies your footstool
122:5	Revelation of the throne of David
144:12	Promise to sons

Asaph

50:7-23	Hear and I will speak
75:2-6	I choose the appointed time
76:11	Message to neighboring lands
81:8	Word to Israel

Sons of Korah

45:13-17	Revelation of the Bride and Bridegroom
46:10	Be still and know that I am God
48:12	Walk about Zion and count her towers

49	Hear this—word to the nations
84:5	Strength to strength
85:10	Love & faithfulness meet together
87	Song for a nation
91	Song of protection

Solomon

72	Revelation of Christ

Ethan

89:3-5	You said
89:19-38	You spoke in a vision

Unknown

33	Sing
91:14	I will rescue
94:8	Word to nations
95:7	They have not known My ways
96:1	Call to worship—nations and creation
98	Call to release the sound of worship
100	Call to worship with joy
104	Revelation of the One
105:15	He speaks protection
112	The blessing and favor of God
113:7	Declaration over the poor
115:12-18	Prophetic blessing

Call to the nations

118:15-17	Prophetic declaration
121:5	The Lord watches over you
128	Blessed

GOVERNING APOSTOLIC PSALMS

David

Asaph

Sons of Korah

Unknown

99:7	Remembering His decrees
113:4	King over nations
114:7	Declaration over the Earth
117	Call to the nations
119:23	In war, remember His decrees
119:54	His decrees are the themes of songs
125:3	Declaration breaking demonic rule
135:15	Declaration over the gods of the nations
147:19	Remembering His decree
148:1-6	Declaration to kingdoms and angels
148:6	God's eternal decrees
149:5-9	Authority of the church

Appendix B

The Vision

Pete Greig

The vision?

The vision is Jesus—obsessively, dangerously, undeniably Jesus.

The vision is an army of young people.

You see bones? I see an army. And they are free from materialism.

They laugh at 9 to 5 little prisons.

They could eat caviar on Monday and crusts on Tuesday.

They wouldn't even notice.

They know the meaning of the Matrix, the way the west was won.

They are mobile like the wind, they belong to the nations. They need no passport. People write their addresses in pencil and wonder at their strange existence.

They are free yet they are slaves of the hurting and dirty and dying.

What is the vision?

The vision is holiness that hurts the eyes. It makes children laugh and adults angry. It gave up the game of minimum integrity long ago to reach for the stars. It scorns the good and strains for the best. It is dangerously pure.

Light flickers from every secret motive, every private conversation.

It loves people away from their suicide leaps, their satan games.

This is an army that will lay down its life for the cause.

A million times a day its soldiers

choose to lose

that they might one day win

the great "well done" of faithful Sons and daughters.

Such heroes are as radical on Monday morning as Sunday night.

They don't need fame from names. Instead they grin quietly upward and hear the crowds chanting again and again: "Come on!"

And this is the sound of the underground

The whisper of history in the making

Foundations shaking

Revolutionaries dreaming once again

Mystery is scheming in whispers

Conspiracy is breathing…

This is the sound of the underground

And the army is discipl(in)ed.

Young people who beat their bodies into submission.

Every soldier would take a bullet for his comrade at arms.

The tattoo on their back boasts "for me to live is Christ, and to die is gain" (Phil. 1:21).

Sacrifice fuels the fire of victory in their upward eyes. Winners.

Martyrs. Who can stop them?

Can hormones hold them back?

Can failure succeed? Can fear scare them or death kill them?

And the generation prays

like a dying man

with groans beyond talking,

with warrior cries, sulphuric tears and

with great barrow loads of laughter!

Waiting. Watching: 24/7/365.

Whatever it takes they will give: Breaking the rules. Shaking mediocrity from its cosy little hide. Laying down their rights and their precious little wrongs, laughing at labels, fasting essentials. The advertisers cannot mold them. Hollywood cannot hold them. Peer-pressure is powerless to shake their resolve at late night parties before the cockerel cries.

They are incredibly cool, dangerously attractive inside. On the outside? They hardly care. They wear clothes like costumes to communicate and celebrate but never to hide.

Would they surrender their image or their popularity?

They would lay down their very lives—swap seats with the man on death row—guilty as hell. A throne for an electric chair.

With blood and sweat and many tears, with sleepless nights and fruitless days,

they pray as if it all depends on God and live as if it all depends on them.

Their DNA chooses Jesus. (He breathes out, they breathe in.)

Their subconscious sings. They had a blood transfusion with Jesus.

Their words make demons scream in shopping centers.

Don't you hear them coming?

Herald the weirdos!

Summon the losers and the freaks.

Here come the frightened and forgotten with fire in their eyes.

They walk tall and trees applaud, skyscrapers bow, mountains are dwarfed by these children of another dimension.

Their prayers summon the hounds of Heaven and invoke the ancient dream of Eden.

And this vision will be. It will come to pass; it will come easily; it will come soon.

How do I know? Because this is the longing of creation itself, the groaning of the Spirit, the very dream of God.

My tomorrow is his today.

My distant hope is his 3D.

And my feeble, whispered, faithless prayer invokes a thunderous, resounding, bone-shaking great "Amen!" from countless angels, from heroes of the faith, from Christ Himself. And He is the original dreamer, the ultimate winner. Guaranteed.

Red Moon Rising, Peter Greig and Dave Roberts (Orlando, FL: Relevant Books, 2005), 119-122.

Appendix C

Recommended Reading

THE KINGDOM OF GOD

When Heaven Invades Earth, Bill Johnson, Destiny Image Publishing, Shippensburg, PA, 2003

Rediscovering the Kingdom, Miles Munroe, Destiny Image Publishing, Shippensburg, PA, 2004

The Unshakable Kingdom & the Unchanging Person, E. Stanley Jones, McNett Press, WA, 1972

WORSHIP

Sound of Heaven, Symphony of Earth, Ray Hughes, MorningStar Publications, Wilkesboro, NC, 2000

The Worship Warrior, Chuck Pierce with John Dickson, Regal Books, Ventura, CA, 2002

The Lost Glory, David Markee, MorningStar Publications, Wilkesboro, NC, 1999

Following the River, Bob Sorge, Oasis House, Lee's Summit, MO, 2004

APOSTLES AND THE APOSTOLIC

Spheres of Authority, Peter Wagner, Wagner Publications, Colorado Springs, CO, 2002

Moving in the Apostolic, John Eckert, Regal Books, Ventura, CA, 1999

The Breaker Anointing, Barbara J. Yoder, Regal Books, Ventura, CA, 2004

Church@Community, Ed Delph, Creation House, Lake Mary, FL, 2005

PROPHETS AND THE PROPHETIC

The Voice of God, Cindy Jacobs, Regal Books, Ventura, CA, 1995

The Seer, Jim W. Goll, Destiny Image Publishers, Shippensburg, PA, 2004

Elijah Task, John & Paula Sandford, Victory House, Tulsa, OK, 1977

Elijah Among Us, John Sandford, Chosen Books, Grand Rapids, MI, 2002

Approaching The Heart of Prophesy, Graham Cook, Punch Press, Winston-Salem, NC, 2006

Prophesy and Responsibility, Graham Cooke, Brilliant Book House, Vacaville, CA, 2007

School of The Prophets Training Manual, Kris Vallotton, Bethel Church, Redding, CA, 2006

Growing in the Prophetic, Mike Bickle, Kingsway Publications, Eastbourne, UK, 1995

You May All Prophesy, Steve Thompson, MorningStar Publications, Wilkesboro, NC, 2000

Releasing the Prophetic Destiny of a Nation, Dutch Sheets & Chuck Pierce, Destiny Image Publishing, Shippensburg, PA, 2005

Londonistan, Melanie Phillips, Encounter Books, New York, NY, 2006

INTERCESSION

Intercessory Prayer, Dutch Sheets, Regal Books, Ventura, CA, 1996

Authority In Prayer, Dutch Sheets, Bethany House, Bloomington, MN, 2006

Possessing The Gates of The Enemy, Cindy Jacobs, Chosen Books, Grand Rapids, MI, 1991

Red Moon Rising, Pete Grieg and Dave Roberts, Relevant Books, Orlando, FL, 2005

The Lost Art of Intercession, James W. Goll, Destiny Image Publishing, Shippensburg, PA, 1997

LIFESTYLE

After God's Own Heart, Mike Bickle, Charisma House, Lake Mary, FL, 2004

A Tale of Three Kings, Gene Edwards, Tyndale House, Wheaton, IL, 1992

Dreaming With God, Bill Johnson, Destiny Image Publishing, Shippensburg, PA, 2006

The Cross Is the Key, Terry Moore, Paradigm Publishing, Lewisville, TX, 2006

Who's Your Daddy Now?, Doug Stringer, Gatekeeper Publishing, Cheshire, CT, 2007

Why Good People Mess Up, John Loren Sandford, Charisma House, Lake Mary, FL, 2007